tidepools

adam tendler

This collection culls from true events, with scenes and dialogue recreated from memory and some names changed to protect privacy. It includes adult language and situations, and is intended for mature readers.

Cover Image: Francesco Simone Savi
Copyright © 2018 Adam Tendler
All rights reserved.
Dissonant States Press, Brooklyn, NY

for F

PART ONE

WHERE CAN ART TAKE YOU?

In a Bronx charter school, working from sub plans, I tell the kids they must design a t-shirt answering the question, "Where Can Art Take You?" My t-shirt example, which most of them copy, of course depicts scenes of my fifty-state tour, because that's where art once took me. And wouldn't it inspire the children? I make palm trees for Hawai'i, which I think will seem exotic, a road, musical notes, a book, a map...

I try to explain my design to these second graders over deafening indifference; students wrestling, pencils flying, girls pulling each others' hair, and in an instant my life feels worthless, my story, my unfinished book, my accomplishments—all fodder, an attempt to look alive-and-well in the eyes of others. By the end of class, I'm tearing off shards of my portrait for bathroom passes.

The newly printed manuscript of my book, tucked in my tote bag, looks like a treasure map of scribbles, arrows, asides, and corrections. The draft I felt so confident in weeks ago, a sample of which I submitted to one of the most powerful agents in New York City, now looks to me like the work of one of today's second graders. The agent has vanished.

Glue explodes in my hands. "They need to make a better top for that," says Ingrid, another art teacher. "Let's say you and I invent a new top, we both become rich, you do your music and I do my art." Ingrid introduces me to the music teacher—cute, straight—but I have nothing to say. To him I'm some dude who calls himself an accomplished musician but who's actually just subbing an art class in the Bronx. So I begin listing places I've lived, and ask him to do the same.

My girlfriend from high school calls me as I leave.

We haven't talked in years, but she has called today to say she likes my blog. "When I read it, it's like you're right here! This is exactly how you sounded in high school!" I thank her. "How's your love life?" A swell of guilt chokes out my words. I still feel like I betrayed her. I'd rather change the subject.

God, how different things would have been if just once in my first twenty-five years I'd simply answered "Yes" to anyone who asked. Or to myself. How might high school have been different, or conservatory, or the fifty-state tour, if I didn't wait all that time to come out, cowardly I still think, in a letter overnighted from Texas to Vermont?

Standing under the Bruckner Expressway, dirt and smoke and brown slush kicked into the air by tractor trailers, I look toward the entry ramp north like its a portal to another world, back to safety, home to Vermont. This 'here,' this New York, is not my home. It can't be. After months of sleeping on floors, drinking till dawn, writing in Starbucks and playing in the Dixon Place lounge in exchange for practice time (when I'm not sneaking into Mannes School), it has shifted into a kind of opponent. Less a city and more a thing to navigate and negotiate lest I suffocate under its impossible weight and magnetic opposition to settling in and calling it home. Voices ask *why don't you just leave?* I've heard that question before, only back in Texas it had a *him* at the end. I didn't leave then, either. Not until he told me to.

I left that day and landed in New York, my bags continuing onward to Vermont. I went straight to my friend Paul's studio on St. Mark's Place. We drank cheap red wine mixed with Diet Coke and went out that night and every night after. When I'd cry, he'd frown and say, "Oh girl," and when we would come home, he'd stay up, smoke and listen to Nina Hagen as I slept on an air mattress at the foot of his bed. I'd wake up and teach a piano lesson uptown, one of the families I found on Craigslist and my only income for months until I started subbing in these schools. Occasionally I mop the floors and grab cases of beer from the basement at Ty's in the West Village. During Pride I guarded their restroom, making sure only one person entered at a time. My tank top read "Bathroom Bouncer."

    Where can art take you?

    Don't ask me. I just work here.

LAST AUGUST IN GAY HELL

8-3-09: Hooked up with a Brazilian party promoter. Hot. Great kisser. He offered me poppers and I said no. Someone told me people do this if they think you're uptight. I didn't feel too slutty because we'd been in touch for months. Stupid me looks at Rob's profile online and sees he's in Chicago. It doesn't affect me the way I'd expect. It's a strange, involved indifference, but still indifference. Then summoned by Chris maybe less than an hour after the Brazilian. Okay, so now I do feel slutty.

8-5-09: I've masturbated through several momentous occasions this year. The Obama inauguration was one of them, and today was another, when I emailed off the first ever complete draft of my book. And somehow I managed to be doing those two things at once. Saw a movie alone tonight, sad and meandering and pointless (the movie), but I liked it. Then I hooked up with Ray just because. Did I do everything I did tonight because I miss Chris? I mean, you can't force someone to want to spend time with you. And why do I want him, anyway? Well, because I'm lonely, of course, and because I take silence personally. It doesn't matter that last month I waited with bags packed by the door for him to pick me up for a trip to Provincetown, not knowing he left without me. Emails from Rob harder to ignore than ever. His spelling is getting worse ("finalie") as are his CAPS choices. Worried. If I could live in a bubble I'd get so much done.

8-6-09: I woke up to a startling realization, or a couple. 1) I have a lot to do 2) It's all good stuff 3) It's okay that no one knows about what I'm doing creatively, or cares 4) Behind me I'm dragging several huge tree trunks in the form of unresolved gay drama that 5) only I can release.

8-8-09: Really? I thought it was the 9th or 10th. Weird date yesterday with a guy who looked like Jesus, only shorter. Chris announces he'll write a book (i.e. someone will write it for him) so he can "make money while he sleeps." This is my rebound? Thinking tonight of the man in Chelsea with all the cats who shushed me when I came.

8-17-09: I need to regiment my time. I made the awful mistake of letting Manhunt back into my life. Thank God no one notices, writes to, or replies to me there. One long, quiet rejection. I can't wait until my one month membership expires.

8-19-09: With each passing day, I'm more convinced that Midtown is hell on earth. I get here and instantly start sweating, instantly feel ugly, pimply, fat. It's nothing but stores, but no real customers. Everyone is in transit. Just now, in Grand Central, I remembered the last time I was there, just after returning from Houston, from Rob in his hospital bed, when he told me to leave (him) minutes before I would meet the man I wasn't supposed to know about and maybe never would have if there hadn't been a car accident and my surprise arrival. Morphine. Intensive care. Those beeps. His resignation when he said it was over. So today I remembered the time I started sobbing into a little doorway on the side of Grand Central, calling Terence, Chuck, Kathy... anyone I knew from Texas because part of me still needed proof that those two years actually happened. Terence answered. It's true: Midtown is hell on earth.

8-21-09: That guy who drinks too much didn't put out. Again. He "likes me too much." I'm just shallow enough to be annoyed. Done. No more watching him swallow beer after beer in the afternoon at Candle Bar near 72nd, where we once witnessed an old man fall drunk and headfirst down the stairs to the bathroom. There he lay at the bottom of the stairwell with his face flat in a pool of blood and his body shaking as we waited for the paramedics. It'll be good to stop dating a bit.

8-24-09: Nearly obsessed today with the idea of contacting Rob. Five months, and I'm barely an ounce better. I don't believe in closure. I've never experienced it with anything or anyone. I realize he knew me best and vice versa. It's that intimacy I miss. Or maybe it's just an intimacy I've invented, romanticized and put into the place of a memory of a relationship that was actually strained and dishonest. I'll never know… but I do stupid things in the meantime to keep the pain of him alive. I make clean breaks from people. They learn to move on, it seems, but I don't. Texted the Brazilian promoter. He replies "Who is this?" Then invites me to a party.

FATAL LIPSTICK

Around the age of twelve I completed a screenplay about a prostitute who, upon contracting AIDS, goes on a sex-fueled rampage targeting her clients, particularly a misguided widower and his, of course, sexually curious son. She kills, maims, frames, and then gets away with everything. I called it FATAL LIPSTICK. It was a bloodbath, but I had a vision. All I needed was a Yes!

I stalked studios, agents, lawyers, anyone in Hollywood whose contact information I could pilfer from Vermont in a pre-internet world. I remember once speaking with Paul Verhoeven's puzzled manager. Yes, the content was juvenile, inaccurate, insensitive, disrespectful, and a nightmare product of early-90s hysteria that saved lives and scared the shit out of everyone else—campier than camp before I even knew what camp was. But it was mine. I nurtured FATAL LIPSTICK not with facts or reason, but with MTV and hundreds of hours of horror movies, courtesy of my father, who for years, on his sporadic visits to Vermont, would bring with him VHS tapes dubbed with three movies each, copied from VCR-to-VCR in extended play mode with no discrimination of content, genre or rating—he must have just rented and copied them at his apartment in New Hampshire—and I'd run these tapes on repeat long after he left. What may have been a total parenting no-no was the essential baking soda to my imagination's vinegar.

But I had always written. There were fantasy books about dinosaurs (LITTLE BILL), memoirs of my vacations (THE FUN TRIP TRILOGY), and graphic novels like the ambitious, over 300-page SCHIZOPHRENIC Part 1 and 2. My schizophrenic, of course, killed people. But my crowning literary achievement was undoubtedly FATAL LIPSTICK. The confidence I had in the work, and the extent to which I pushed it, was what would become pure and typical Tendler insanity; the urgency of "I have something here."

But by the time I entered high school and started thinking about pursuing the piano more seriously, FATAL LIPSTICK had all-but-faded into memory. Yes, I could still see it frame-by-frame, but I'd given up on harassing agents at CAA. It became just another vanquished project strewn across a battlefield of so many others, and so many to come. It was around this time that fate struck its final nail into the coffin of FATAL LIPSTICK. On a whim, my best friend Roy, our friend Rebecca, and I all decided to stage a reading of the script in the bed of Roy's father's pickup truck as he drove us to Pizza Putt an hour north. Kids doing kids stuff, right? Right. She would read the prostitute, Roy would read the dad, and I'd be the bi-curious son (obviously).

So there we were, tucked illegally in a covered truck-bed speeding up Interstate 89, trying with all our might to perform FATAL LIPSTICK, but we just couldn't. We were laughing too hard. We barely made it halfway through. Yet at the same time, part of me, not laughing, surveyed the scene like a satellite taking everything in at once before spitting out a message, a question, injected deep into the bottom of my brain where it remains to this day. *Can you ever trust yourself again?*

All at once, I saw the faces of those people to whom I'd sent FATAL LIPSTICK: the managers, the agents, the "connected" boyfriends of my cosmopolitan sisters. I wasn't ashamed of the content, per se—that came later—but just of being so goddamn wrong.

Every artist, I think, has to blend a certain bit of caution with his or her desire to risk. Even at our most audacious, we have a kind of surveillance camera hanging over our heads asking, "Are you sure? Are you sure?" Sometimes I'll chew an idea until it's all but unrecognizable. It's a defense, of course, because unless I poke at something ad infinitum, it runs the risk of aging, of becoming a thing of the past. And what happens to those things? You take them out after a couple years and laugh your way to Pizza Putt. That's what.

It strikes me that the book I'm writing now about my fifty state tour is but a most basic literary evolution between my childhood stories about a lost dinosaur, the trilogy about my vacations, the comic book about a homicidal schizophrenic, and FATAL LIPSTICK, my screenplay about a prostitute on a killing spree. So allow me to present now, the story of a pianist who realizes in the end that there is no danger like the danger of ambition. The story of my life. It's a bloodbath, but I have a vision. All I've ever needed is a Yes.

GRENADE

I tossed my G.I. Joe costume from the previous night's Halloween party on top of some dirty clothes in the corner of the guest room. I was in Reno to play John Cage's *Sonatas and Interludes* for prepared piano. Well, the Reno concert would happen in a week, but I had a performance of the same piece the following day in Juneau, Alaska. So I'd fly to Alaska from Reno, play the show the next afternoon, and come back to Reno the following morning to wait a couple days until the next concert. So why come to Reno so early? Well, for that Halloween party, of course!

At gate C6 of Reno International Airport, reclining before a wall-length window, a male voice crackled across the terminal loudspeakers: "Adam Taylor, please return to ticketing. Adam Taylor." *Adam Taylor?*

What a coincidence, I thought. And then it hit me, and it hit me all at once. I'd failed to take something out of my bag that morning, something I had meant to incorporate into my Halloween costume the night before but forgot. The grenade.

Yes, a real grenade. But not, like, a live grenade, just a grenade shell. I bought it for five dollars at an Army Navy store in Vermont. In fact, I'd traveled with it quite a bit before, from Vermont to Houston, and from Houston (and back) through this very airport one year earlier when I went to Burning Man. And of course I'd also had it in my bag during this trip to Reno. Never a problem. But in that moment I knew my luck had run out.

Inside my bag I also had packed a black and red box emblazed with an insignia of a dragon, and inside that box I kept the preparation materials for *Sonatas and Interludes*. Nuts, bolts, screws, rubber hosing, shards of plastic, all wrapped in Ziploc bags, tiny envelopes, or crumpled paper baggies. No, this didn't look good. I crept toward the ticket counter. "Adam Taylor?" I asked. "Not... Adam Tendler?"

"Hold on a second." The attendant sank beneath the counter with the phone cord following him like a fishing line. Crouching there, he turned his back to me and clutched the phone to his ear, a finger pressed into the other, like a hostage negotiator. Then he rose and began surveying the gate area as if I'd evaporated, as if I wasn't the reason he'd plunged to the floor in the first place.

"Adam *Tendler*?" he called out to the room.

"I'm right here."

"You have to come with me."

What began as a solemn procession toward security evolved for me into a desperate, rapid-fire series of explanations. "See, it's funny..."

We continued down the escalator and into the

ticketing lobby. The mood there had changed. I noticed the sunny young woman who, just minutes before had checked me in, complimented my glasses, and asked for my ID (only after I reminded her) now swallowed by TSA agents, her smile gone. Clusters of police and airport officials were huddled around the room whispering.

"Adam Tendler?" A woman with curly hair stepped forward. "Want to tell us what's in your bag?" Men with mustaches and firearms flanked her on both sides.

"Well," I hesitated. "There's a lot of stuff in there. Clothes, some shoes, but I think I know what you're talking about. This is about the grenade." No one said yes or no, but their bodies twitched at the word, the acknowledgment of the thing no one really wanted to name. I went ahead and told them about Halloween, and how I intended the grenade for the costume the night bef—

"But there's a pin in it," one of the men interrupted.

"Yes."

"And chicken wire strung through it. Is that part of your costume, too?"

"Oh, that's just so I can wear it as a belt."

A few seconds of silence.

Another man spoke. "Are nails coming out of it?"

His colleagues looked at him as if he'd just spoiled some surprise, something I was supposed to reveal on my own. But his question actually made no sense, which made me nervous. "Nails coming out of it?" I asked. It's a particularly vulnerable feeling when all you have is the truth on your side. Now I began to sweat, and the parts of my face not covered with a thick black beard went flush. "No, it doesn't have nails coming out of it," I began slowly. "But there are screws and bolts in my bag."

"Why?"

"Ever heard of John Cage?"

"I have!" chirped the attendant who guided me back down from the gate. "I love John Cage. Prepared piano!"

It was a miracle. "Yes!" I said, flooded with relief, pointing to him, my eyes screaming *back me up here!* "I'm a pianist, and I will use those materials in my bag to prepare the piano for tomorrow's concert in Alaska." I started shuffling through my carry-on to bring out the score and show them the table of preparations, the chart in Cage's score that says where on the strings to insert each object.

"There also appears to be liquid. Plastic bottles with nozzles and rubber encasements, all filled with liquid, like a gel or cream. You mind telling us what those are?"

I sort of froze, answering in a voice disconnected

and shaking, "Those are enemas. Medicine." By their puzzled gazes, I could tell that my answer had hardly sufficed. "I have colitis. Those are for if I get sick."

Well, that was humiliating. But at least I'd explained everything. The hardware was for my concert, the enemas for my colitis, and the grenade was for my costu—

"So if we go into your bag we'll find a costume?"

"What?"

...I tossed my G.I. Joe costume from the previous night's Halloween party on top of some dirty clothes in the corner of the guest room...

Shit.

"No," I said.

"No?"

"No," I sank back, defeated. "The rest of my costume is back at my friend's place, where I stayed last night. I forgot to bring the grenade out of my luggage for the party. That's why it's still there."

"Let's call it 'the item,'" said the curly-haired woman beside me through clenched teeth, eyeing the growing crowd of anxious spectators.

"So there's nothing in your bag to prove that you ever had a costume?"

"Listen," I argued. "You can take the gren—... the *item* and throw it away. I don't even want it! It's just an accessory, a prop!"

A young officer interjected. "Don't matter at this point." He flipped through a small pad. "You've already violated Title 49, Code of Federal Regulations."

"Sorry?"

"Subpart B, Subsection 1540."

"What's he saying?"

"1-1-C... parenthesis three."

"Parenthesis three?"

"Props and replicas," he answered diligently.

"Prohibited."

A new interrogator appeared, manifesting a digital camera from his pouch, squealing, "I can show you it! You wanna' see it?" Then he turned to me. "You need the screws for what? They go into the what?"

One of the men groaned, "You know, Larry, you come here late, you start asking about all these things we've already gone over…"

And as they argued, the curly-haired woman took me aside by the elbow. "See, our experts need to clear the bag before you go on the plane. The officials who have your bag now aren't authorized to open it."

"But the…" I nodded toward the man with the camera.

"They can't open it," she reiterated, "in case it detonates."

I felt woozy. "So where are the experts?"

"On their way."

My legs felt like they might run away without me.

"You'll miss your flight," she said. "They'll reroute you to LA, connect you to Seattle, you'll stay there overnight, and then you'll fly to Juneau tomorrow. When is your concert?"

"Tomorrow." I rubbed my eyes. "Tomorrow afternoon." Even if I arrived in the morning, it would be a pinch. Preparing the piano for *Sonatas and Interludes* generally took me about two hours, and I hadn't practiced in days. "Can I just go to Alaska with my concert materials and then you send the bag with my clothes later?"

"No, because if they find something, we'll need you here." She paused. "To arrest you."

"Right, of course."

Twenty minutes went by, during which several men gave me their cards, asked my contact information, inquired about my concert (hey, outreach is outreach), and examined my ID with a magnifying glass and an array of lights and sensors.

"So this is your address?" one asked. "Texas?"

"Yes...I mean. No...Well, I mean, sure, you can put that address down... Oh wait, no! Don't. That's not a good one. Here, I'll tell you a better one..."

"And when and where did you purchase the item?" he asked.

"Over a year ago in Vermont. I've said that already."

He scribbled in his pad, muttering, "a couple days ago, here..."

"ARE YOU TRAVELING ALONE!" barked a towering woman in a deep baritone, her makeup smeared into a rainbow of fluorescents. I'd never seen her before. She charged into the middle of the group of officers. I told her that indeed I was traveling alone. Her face melted into a grimace of despair and confusion.

"Then how did you *GET HERE?!*"

"A friend drove me."

Someone pulled her away, as if breaking up a fight. One man spoke into his walkie-talkie. "Just tell them to pull the bomb squad around back and drop the guys off so pedestrians aren't alarmed, and keep any media out by the…"

I turned to the woman who remained by my side. "We've been waiting for the bomb squad?"

"Listen, you have the perfect storm in that bag," she said. "TSA looks for a device, an agent, and things to connect them all together. Between your item, your liquids, and your box of hoses and hardware, you fit the bill for a bona fide threat. I know you're not a… but…"

I didn't know if I might faint or cry.

"Let me see if I can help," she whispered, and walked over to the nearest group of agents, leaning in and speaking to them like a quarterback. I could just barely make out her voice. "If his bag is cleared when he's at the gate, then he can go right on. So someone should go up with him now." No one moved. So she repeated herself.

"What about his bag?" one man growled. "It needs to make the flight."

"It just goes on a truck. Takes a minute."

Dead silence, and then the men resumed their conversation, pushing her out of their circle. They'd made their decision long ago, it seemed, and she sulked toward me when a voice shouted something indiscernible through on her walkie-talkie. She held it to her ear and then looked at me with wild, happy eyes. "They cleared you! RUN!"

The same attendant who had accompanied me from the gate appeared again by my side, and without saying as much as a goodbye to anyone, we scrambled out of the lobby. "You know," he huffed as we ran up the escalator, "I came with you before because I thought you might bail if I let you go alone!"

The gate came within view. I still technically had five minutes until departure, but I could still hear men screaming at the attendant through his walkie-talkie to give up, saying the flight needed to push out of the gate.

"We're just coming up to security!" he panted back.

A voice sputtered from his walkie-talkie. "If you're at security, then you can't make it. They're closing the door. They can't be delayed."

Fuck you, I wanted to say. *I* can't be delayed.

There was no line at security. Maybe we had a chance. The attendant sprinted through and turned around, bending his knees and egging me on like a man watching his horse at the races. I took my laptop out of the bag, tossed my shoes on the conveyor belt and ran through the sensor, boarding pass crinkled in my hand.

BEEP BEEP BEEP. My pockets! I ran back, threw my cell phone and wallet into one of the bowls stacked next to the belt, and lunged through the sensor once more. Finally arriving again at the foot of Gate C6, the attendant and I were greeted only by exaggerated frowns. "We tried," cooed a girl in uniform. I looked out the window and could see the pilot and crew inside the cockpit. The plane remained there for a few minutes before backing away.

I asked the attendant next to me if perhaps I could get a hotel voucher my overnight Seattle layover, since after all, this whole thing had just been one big misunderstanding. "I'm sorry," he answered. "We don't have a policy for pianists with grenades. But," he lit up, "I'm excited for your concert! It's on Wednesday?"

"7 p.m."

LAST SUMMER WHEN I WAS A PIMP

Last summer when I was a pimp, I made sixty dollars before quitting. The idea wasn't mine, actually, but that of my first client, a man in Brooklyn who posted a Craigslist ad in the employment classifieds asking for someone, anyone, to help him hook up with girls while keeping his involvement in the process to a minimum.

I was low on options with a bank account near zero. So I responded to the ad and promptly received a response. Perhaps it was my track record—nationally touring pianist, experienced nonprofit director, teacher, composer—he must've figured the least I could do was find a guy a date. And from what I read, it seemed that simple. He presented himself in his reply as a nice older gentleman tired of trolling the Internet and finding nothing but hustlers, fakes, floosies, and spam. He was willing to pay for two things: a girl's "time," and the service of anyone who could help facilitate it. Twenty bucks an hour. Sure!

It had been just a couple days since I'd moved into a two-floor share on 5th Street between Avenues A and B, my first official New York City apartment since my Texas exile. Since the breakup. Since the car accident. Since flying to Texas and heading straight to the hospital, still under the illusion that I could live in two places at once, have a relationship in two places at once, and in fact feeling ready to re-commit to a life back in Texas because, for one, there had been this car accident, and also New York just wasn't working. Instead, I gathered my things that same day under the drugged orders of my suddenly-ex, but not before meeting my surprise replacement. "Hello." And by the next evening I was a New Yorker.

So, yeah. This was my first real place since *that*.

In between, it had just been floors and couches.

The bottom level of this apartment was actually underground, and there, in a windowless room down a dark hallway, I threw a mattress on a damp sandy floor (or were those insect eggs?) and called it home. I remember it as the room where one day I woke up from a rare afternoon nap to find out that Michael Jackson had died, and soon my roommates, three straight guys, discovered me in the kitchen weeping to "Man in the Mirror."

Those three NYU graduates hated locking doors and loved sports, all day juggling different live feeds from ESPN between the TV and various laptops. The walls were adorned with sports memorabilia and classic rock album art, the living room floor covered with artificial grass. What they thought when I emerged from my room each day with bicycle shorts and a "Boys R Toys" cut-off, singing Kylie Minogue at the kitchen table while working on my book, my score, or my job search, is beyond me, but they needed a roommate to finish out the lease, and I needed a place to stay, a place that wasn't a friend's couch, a place that wouldn't remind me of the breakup, the breakdown, of Texas.

Journal entry from 5-26-09: *...there was an awkward silence last night at drinks when I admitted that I look forward to sleeping each night because it means I'll dream, and see, and interact with him again.*

I was still something of a phantom, adjusting to the hetero atmosphere of that brand new bachelor pad when I confessed to my roommates that not only was I a pianist writing a book, composing a song cycle, teaching private students and barbacking at Ty's, but that I was also moonlighting as a pimp. There was no other term I could think of to describe my role. Send girls to so-and-so and receive a commission. "Cool," they said.

Journal from 6-3-09: *...I start tomorrow! Basically, he wants me to place Craigslist ads in search of "nice girls" who might "need a little cash." "Not pros," he says. Ha. What in the WORLD?! Pen dying... New pen. We talked on the phone today, and he sounded like a character from The Sopranos. Said he's going to Jersey for a couple days after tomorrow...also owns several bars :-/ But he uses his real email address (I guess), sounds nice enough...so I'm not really worried. Oh, but if he kills me: his name is [omitted] (←OMG "Tony!!"), and his number is 917-[omitted]. This is where I'm meeting him tomorrow: [omitted].*

Journal from the next day, 6-4-09: *...So there I am in Brooklyn, and suddenly it seems not like an office where we'll be meeting, but rather an apartment on the third* *floor of a rundown waterfront building. We still have a couple minutes before our designated meeting time when a guy disappears through the front door, but not without first looking at me with a kind of knowing, expectant look from beneath his baseball cap. I start asking myself, why am I being summoned from a Craigslist ad for help with placing Craigslist ads? Why did Tony ask if I planned to bring my computer? Why did another similar Craigslist ad show up when I Googled Tony's email address, the other ad being for someone to help him with his computer and stereo (also $20 hr).*

So now I'm sure that this is some elaborate racket summoning the unemployed and impressionable to a nondescript location in Brooklyn to be... I don't know... robbed, beaten, murdered. I begin pacing on the sidewalk. It's not necessarily for fear of my safety, but more for my work. I haven't properly backed up the newest edit of my book on the laptop, which I did indeed bring with me. In fact, it's the only other thing in my bag besides this very journal, the one containing Tony's address and contact info. It's like I've collected all the evidence and everything I care about, and brought it here. But still, I've come this far, so I call the number Tony gave me and say I'm downstairs. He cheerfully answers and directs me two doors down from the rundown building I've been pacing in front of to an inviting, spacious office front. A secretary types away inside, and when I walk in she says she's been expecting me.

Tony was sixty-something years old and looked like George Jones, wearing a Polo shirt and tinted glasses, his rusty golden hair parted to the side. I immediately described my plan. We'd create a new email address with one, agreed-upon password. He'd provide me with pictures, information, and so on, and I would act as him on the web.

"We can communicate over this shared email address, basically sending emails to ourselves," I explained. "And this is also the email address I'll use when placing our ads and communicating with other ads and with the girls. So if you wish, you can check in and monitor what I'm doing, and once we have someone who seems promising, I'll bow out and you can take over to set up the actual date."

As our first order of business, right there in the office he emailed me series of pictures—pictures of him on vacation, him at parties, him during family gatherings. "Maybe I can edit some of these," I suggested, "so we're not sending images of your loved ones." He agreed with a shrug. "And let's figure out the wording of the ad you want to post."

I surmised Tony had some ideas already prepared, because he answered quickly. "Nice, wealthy, older successful gentleman is willing to help with..."

"Generous," I interrupted.

"What?"

"In these kinds of ads, the word 'generous' is pretty much understood as a code for 'willing to pay.'"

"How do you know?"

"I just... do," I said. Craigslist, of course, was a wasteland of closet-cases, and once-upon-a-time I knew it and its language quite well.

"Maybe you can find a nice girl for yourself in the process," he said with a smirk. "I don't know your type but..."

I laughed and waved the topic away.

"... well anyway my type is voluptuous," he continued. "And I like 'em young. Not like, really young. But if they're, say, nineteen...*eighteen*!" His eyes lit up. "And real submissive-like. Someone who will let me be in charge, be the boss. Someone humble. With a sparkle."

He was lost in this thought for a second as I scrawled notes in the journal. *humble, with sparkle...*

He also seemed to be searching in this pause to see if perhaps he'd gone too far, if his laundry list of preferences had pushed me into any traceable zone of discomfort. They hadn't. Then he assigned words to his thought: "I don't want to get, you know, too graphic, but seeing as what you're doing for me…"

"This is a free zone," I answered. "Say what you want."

"So yeah, I like shape," he went on without hesitation. "Some real shape to them." He made a gesture, like cradling an ass in front of his chest. "Like I said, voluptuous. But not black."

"Hm?"

"I don't want any black girls. Asian maybe. They'll be submissive."

I wanted to puke, but with my sense of decency a

faint memory, I kept scribbling, and before I knew it, two hours had gone by. Tony slipped me two twenties, invited me to send some musician friends to one of his bars to play, and if I ever wanted a gig myself, "Don't hesitate to ask."

I went home to work, and discovered there were indeed a lot of pros out there—not necessarily prostitutes, but rather countless personal ads that connected to other sites and galleries. Girls who at first seemed to be human were revealed after an email or two to be bots. The furthest I could ever wish to go with them might be a live "show" via some sad, crimson-hued cyberpurgatory of a porn website. No thanks. As for the real girls—and there were a couple—they uniformly wanted money for their time, which was fine, but they also didn't fit Tony's preferences. Craigslist, it seemed, was nothing more than a tangled nest of call-girl agencies, webcam sites, and real-life goblins. That is, if you were unlucky enough to be straight.

Yes, if I'd had at my disposal the ease, efficiency, and urgency of a gay online hookup site, not rickety old Craigslist or the hooker-swarmed AdultFriendFinder, then I'd have had Tony set up in minutes. I shook my head, fell back in my chair and looked up from the laptop to my roommates. "How do you guys do it?"

"Bars."

I slumped forward, thinking of a friend who once told me he cruised a guy across 45th street, and the guy cruised him back, and on and on they walked, cruising each other, meandering westward three avenues before finally separating and returning to their respective homes, where within seconds they found each other online, chatted there, and then met up.

Bars. How quaint.

A week went by, and though I'd accrued over five hours of work, I had nothing. I emailed Tony a bill for my time, but he never paid me, and, feeling like a failure, I didn't push it. Our communication faded out as quickly as it had begun. I did, however, post my new service on Craigslist as an experiment, and received one hit.

Once again, I tried to help the guy. The task was to find a girl who would pretend to meet him and his wife at random in public, and then things would evolve from there. I put in one hour, have no idea what came of it, but he faithfully sent me a twenty-dollar bill in a white envelope. And that was that, my brief career as a pimp.

But while I may now have a piano studio of thirty pupils, am performing more, and am no longer in the sex trade, some things remain the same. I'm still trying to perform, to compose, to publish my book. Still broke. And still not quite sure how to answer the question, "What do you do?" In New York, it's a touchy question. There's often a disparity between what so many of us do, and then what we *do*, and I find myself often at once inspired and revolted by those few souls who, by some miracle, have actually aligned the two. How dare they? Do they remember the days when they hustled? The days when they pimped?

THE DAY I MET F

Journal from 11/15/09: ...went for a run this afternoon down to Battery Park and back. At the end, I decided to finish with a little jog onto the Christopher St. Pier. As I ran, I came across a cute guy sitting on a bench, sort of bearish but more compact, wearing tons of red—eek!—but our eyes met, and as I ran by our gaze never broke. I even turned around after I passed him, and he was <u>still</u> looking. I actually burst out laughing. Wow! Truly a violent cruising. Then I considered he might have just been mortified by my outfit (including my "Boys R Toys" cut-off). At any rate, I stopped at the end of the pier, gazing out on the Hudson, and coached myself: If I'm not looking online, how else can I expect to meet people? Go talk to him! (Then again, I tried this on Friday with someone I thought was cruising me at the SNAXX party.

Disaster.) Anyway, I walked back over and asked this guy on the bench what he was reading, since he'd brought out a book, and it was Larry Kramer's *Faggots*, which I just bought myself, same edition and everything. So we talked about that, and about The Strand bookstore, and then naturally I started talking about disaster capitalism and Naomi Klein. I explained that I didn't have my cell and couldn't take his number, and he looked at me completely unaffected. "So..." I said, "DO YOU WANT MINE?!" I thought I'd never hear from him again, but then he texted me a half-hour later. His name is Francesco.

PART TWO

LIKE THIS

"There is no New York scene, only Facebook," I declared to an actor tonight at a bar. He'd mentioned a young composer and, as best as I could tell, asked me if I knew his work. I started talking shit, leaning toward him, my Jack and Coke sloshing in its glass. A bass line shook the wood-paneled floor, and everyone around us seemed to be shouting to a friend staring into the blue glow of a phone. Sweat-glazed bodies, New York City under a heat dome. My own shiny face, at first simply flush with jealousy, turned red with embarrassment when I realized that the actor had in fact just told me he was *working* with that composer, and that he thought the two of us should meet. I've actually met that composer several times and we have all the same friends.

It's nearly impossible to make a case for yourself as an artist in the 21st century when self-expression is everyone's primary form of entertainment.

Found in my email drafts folder: *very drunk. and just found and took codeine. if i die before i wake, let it be known that i don't believe in legacy, and that everything is a lie. i don't believe in popularity, and i've loved the wrong way since as far back as i allow myself to remember. if i die before i wake, at least i'll be with my dog, who died today. i had him since i was fourteen. the saddest thing about death, i think, is leaving family behind. it's the only, and i mean only, reason i didn't jump off the top of a rooftop bar tonight as people waited in hoards below to get in, and as those who did, like me, sat there, smoking, pretending to be famous.*

I seriously considered quitting this week—Facebook, that

is, which I don't do as much as watch. But like any addict, I quickly convinced myself that not only do I enjoy it (which I don't) but that I need it (which I don't). Joining was the biggest mistake I've made in the last two years, but I'm afraid leaving would be my next.

Over lunch on Fire Island last week, I brought up the subject of my previous struggles with ulcerative colitis. As the conversation evolved, I overheard the guest of one of our roommates ask him under his breath what colitis was, and the roommate, a doctor himself, responded in a whispered snicker: "Let's wait till after lunch." I interrupted whatever I was saying and sneered across the table: "It's when your immune system wants to eat your soul, but will settle for your colon."

I've never seen a guide dog who didn't look miserable.

I learned of my dog's death while working in a summer camp on a field trip with over a dozen five-year-olds on the hottest day of the year. *103°, feels like 114°* read my phone. For the sake of the children, I had to repress any acknowledgment of the news, but I fear this repression has carried me over the last couple of days, and might extend into the future. I want to explode the sadness out of me, but can't. I only teared up once, listening to my mother and stepfather sobbing on the other end of the phone while I myself stared at pictures of the dog and me, on Facebook.

F said recently, during a fight, that I'm like a child in that I always do what I want with no consideration of anyone else. This is funny because I think of myself as the one person I know who almost never does what he wants, and who acts only in accordance with what I think will make other people happy. My natural equilibrium is misery, it seems. Maybe that's okay. Last week when I asked him if he'd rather make love or eat the cheese sandwich he was preparing, I watched like a cuckold as he devoured it.

SAN FRANCISCO

My friend from New York, also visiting San Francisco this week, sinks beside me into the couch and we begin talking about Ned Rorem. "I can't believe the gaps," he says, referring to the pacing of Rorem's Diaries. "How he can skip a couple years between one page and the next."

"Well, we all have gaps," I say, allowing a pause before asking the inevitable question. "Am I in a gap? Is *this* a gap?"

He responds in less than a second. "No."

I nod, staring ahead. I suppose that's what I needed to hear. Then he adds, "But last year, yes."

EDITORIAL TO THE NEW YORK TIMES THAT I NEVER SENT

While hardly a musical anarchist, and not at all a sadist, I have to say that I read with delight the Times's lament about the disturbance of other people practicing their instruments elsewhere in the Mannes School of Music during a well-known pianist's recent concert. It must have been quite a disheartening experience, hearing that "noise" in the background, especially considering the exceptional amount of ink The Times used in notifying its readers of the concert beforehand. Perhaps some of the students at the conservatory didn't find the occasion so momentous?

As a concert pianist myself who has performed internationally as well as in all fifty states, I've competed with everything from coffee grinders to enemies of modern music. As a pianist living in your immediate vicinity, I've competed with car horns, subways, fellow musicians, a dismissive pubic, and an oblivious arts press. Your paper is particularly allergic to my activities. The other day, when I attempted to practice a soft Ned Rorem waltz at 2 p.m. in my apartment, a neighbor reported me to the Housing Authority.

It occurs to me that I myself have been one of those practicing nuisances at Mannes. When I first came to the city, before I had a piano or anywhere to practice, I would bustle past security with a phone pressed to my ear and scores shoved under my arm, pretending to talk to someone and appearing to be too busy to stop. This was just so I could practice, and for a while it worked. Practice I would, until an actual student kicked me out of the room. Soon, security intervened and stopped me at the doors. A nuisance, indeed.

In many ways, I owe a good portion of my life in

music to the work of The New York Times and the pianist you reviewed—both served to inspire me in my formative years—so let me emphasize that it's with the highest respect that I welcome you both, in this indifferent city and unforgiving century, to New York.

SPECIAL

I played the saxophone for a year when I was ten. I might have been good at it, too, but already played the piano and opted, impractically, to stick with that for the school band, mostly doubling tuba parts while sitting on the side of the room behind a giant keyboard propped atop an amp, drunk with power. It was a terrible scenario for the bandleader, because in those days my top priority was to entertain. With countless samples at my fingertips, I would create improvisatory outros to all of the band's mishaps, or trigger a laugh track to someone's joke. As for my teacher, I would accompany his reprimands with a walking bass, or often, as he addressed the room with an instruction, would turn the volume very low and press the helicopter sound and watch as people's eyes darted to the window in confusion.

Reduced to madness, the poor man would scream from the podium, and I'd come away from band rehearsal sort of judging my performance, scanning through it and determining: did the seagull 'bit' land, or did I do better with the machine gun fire? I would wonder if that day's disruptions felt artfully justified, or just mean-spirited. And so on. What's amazing, looking back, is that I remember feeling guilty almost every day about my behavior. I'd promise myself that next time I wouldn't get so carried away, that I would work with my teacher and avoid trying to make everyone laugh. And then of course, the next day would come and I'd crumble under the temptation. An atomic bomb blasts during a John Philip Sousa march.

The bandleader actually married the band assistant. She was also an occasional substitute at the school and mother (from a previous marriage) of one of my classmates. She had wire-rimmed glasses and gray hair pulled back into a ponytail. She really hated me, but I figured it was less my bandroom decorum and more because every time we went on a field trip I'd inadvertently tell my mom the wrong pick-up time and this unlucky woman would have to wait with me at the school for an extra hour till she came. What a mess.

One day—and it's all still kind of foggy—I think everyone had been told not to make any noise, and of course I made a sound with the keyboard. Looking more determined than in the past, she barreled over. "Who do you think you are?" she shrieked as the band teacher watched on, defenseless. "Do you think you're special?" Before I could answer she said, "You're not. You're not special." She repeated it several times. "You're not special. You're not special." Over and over she said it. "Now *you* say it!" she demanded. The rest of the room watched. "I want you to say it! Say 'I'm not special.'" No one was laughing. Over her shoulder, I could see her son squirming in his seat. "Say it! Say that you're not special!"

"I'm not special," I said. And I don't remember much else after that.

LOUNGE PIANO GANGBANG

I've never thought being a whore would bother me. I mean, like, an actual whore. I think I could separate love and sex—who hasn't?—and not overthink the whole compensation element. Many of my friends in the arts actually make their rent with sex work, and they've occasionally argued the lifestyle's merits to me. But I digress, because the real matter at hand is that I'm on a subway platform with sore hands and dress pants on, thinking to myself: So I'm a whore, and this is what it feels like. I just spent two hours playing piano for money at a Sak's Fifth Avenue private party celebrating associates who have sold a million dollars or more in merchandise.

At first I was elated by the invitation. "Wow, I'm getting referred," I thought. "And I don't even *do* lounge music!" That's precisely when I should have stopped. Indeed, I *don't* do lounge music. And then more red flags popped up. The guys in charge wanted to meet me. Then hear me. Years of audition trauma came flooding back, but I agreed to have them meet me at Soho House in the Meatpacking District where, twice a week, I do play two-hour marathons of ambient treatments of pop music. Still, not really lounge music.

So picture it. I'm deep into a ten-minute rendition of "Like a Virgin" when these two men in suits appear. Now I really start to play out. These are the guys, I figure. I start playing inside the piano, delving into the psycho-sexual-subterranean universe of "Like a Virgin." Eventually, still playing, I feel a tap on my shoulder. They introduce themselves. I stop.

"Did you find the place all right?" I ask.

"No, not really."

And as we go on introducing ourselves, they hint

ever more emphatically that whatever I was just doing, was definitely NOT what they had in mind for the party. "We want, you know, show tunes, standards for people to sing along."

I gulped.

"Do you take requests?"

No, I thought. "Sure!"

"Good, because really we just want the party to be *fun*," one of them said. It's a word that would haunt me for the next couple of weeks and all the way to tonight. "Fun. We want Fun."

I don't know why I didn't say no right then and there, why I didn't say, "Thanks anyway but this isn't really a match," and then send these gentlemen on their merry way to The Monster where half the guys in the room have libraries of 'fun' material in their heads and hands. Those were the guys for the job, really. Why go along with this?

Money. I wanted $250 for two hours of playing. Simple. So I accepted the gig, and the three weeks since then have been hell. I've been wracking my brain over how to be fun, and it hasn't helped that every couple days I've received some kind of email from those same two guys with a less-than-discreet emphasis on how fun the event should be. Fun.

I can't do this, I thought, going to Vermont and sifting through all the cheesy sheet music in the family library that I could find and borrowing Broadway books from friends here in New York. Or, I also thought, maybe it'll be amazing. I've been known to blow events like this out of proportion in my mind. You should've seen me preparing for a Christmas party earlier this winter. Holy shit. I was beside myself with anxiety, practicing carols in a cold sweat. And then the event was, well... fun! A blast, really. Maybe this, too, would be a breeze. Maybe I'd have fun.

It was mere minutes after I arrived tonight when I realized this indeed wouldn't be a blast nor a breeze. Not by a long shot. "Do you have a set list?" asked one of the planners the second I sat at the piano, examining my books and a rough list of pop songs that couldn't have been satisfying to him nor anyone else. Throughout the night, people would pick it up, puzzle over it, and then squawk openly about not recognizing the songs. "What are these, songs or makeup colors!" one girl shrieked.

But I'm getting ahead of myself. "I have an idea of what I'll do," I lied, hoping the planners would just leave.

They didn't, and the night became less about fun and more about someone named Suzanne. Yes, Suzanne, a woman whose role and identity remained a mystery, but who I apparently needed to fear because it seemed, frankly, everyone else did. "When Suzanne comes in, really let 'er rip." "Suzanne will want to sing." "Suzanne will dig through your music." I wanted to ask: Who the fuck is Suzanne?

"We want you to start with something peppy and fun," said the other planner, suddenly leafing through my books. "Can you do...uh, 'The Very Thought of You,' only more upbeat? Peppy? Fun?"

"Sure!" Already this was my nightmare. Seated at the rented, barely-tuned piano, which was the centerpiece of the room, I was noodling around the keyboard when the same guy who had just prepared my opening number for me shouted across the room, "HERE THEY COME!" meaning, I guessed, the sales associates, the partygoers... maybe Suzanne? Appropriately panicked by his tone, I started to play, and so the tone was set for the next two hours.

Minutes later, Suzanne arrived to much aplomb. One of the planners whizzed by. "This is the moment! Suzanne's here! Give it all you got!" So I just banged out

"The Very Thought of You" again, only louder.

For the rest of the evening, any fleeting moment of comfort was instantly dashed again and again as some administrator whispered a demand in my ear, or rather, a vague suggestion. I can't tell you how many times this happened, nor could I necessarily tell you why. The guests all seemed to be having…fun. It was only the administrators who seemed to be losing their minds.

"Can you do doo wop?" one minion asked. I looked at her blankfaced.

"Like, what? A barbershop quartet on the piano?" I asked. At another point, this same person came over while I played and shivered, as if afraid, "Okay so we need to spruce it up! Is this 'Celebration' song you have on your list like…" and then she began singing, "*Celebrate good times, come on!*" I didn't have the heart to tell her that, no, in fact it was a Madonna song. In any event, I began to play, terribly, the handful of chords suggesting the song she hoped for. Suzanne appeared. A hulking, bird-like figure, she held the mic and announced, just to me, "I'm about to speak."

"Okay?"

"Can you play 'New York, New York'?"

I got through no more than ten seconds before she cut me off. "That's good." She addressed the crowd of million dollar moneymakers, though I'm not sure she thanked a single one of them for anything, then passed the mic to yet another man who told these people why they'd "proved the recession wrong." God in heaven.

No sooner did this pomp come to end than I found Suzanne at my side demanding to sing, but she wasn't sure just what song. I suggested a couple. "TOO SLOW," she snapped. Then she decided, for some reason, on "Makin' Whoopee" and sang, mic and everything, swaying back and forth behind me—a menacing presence—as everyone in the room watched, smiles frozen. Then she sang "Misty." A circle formed. People cheered.

Then Suzanne disappeared, but not before urging everyone to come ask me to play a song. "He'll play anything you want," she said. "No I won't," I actually managed to reply, and my only interactions with her from then on came via shrouded complaints from her associates about my playing, and make no mistake, they came every couple minutes.

Imagine if you will, that you throw a party and someone keeps coming up to you to say they don't like the lighting—no other information, but perhaps the lighting could be more… fun—and then they go away as you adjust the lights only to reappear thirty seconds later to say the same exact thing. Then imagine this going on for two hours. That's what this was like for me, except lights are lights and music is mus—

"How about 'Hey Big Spender'? Can you play

that?" Others were now following Suzanne's suggestion, folks in cocktail attire requesting mostly Frank Sinatra songs that I'd never heard of. A dehumanizing exchange would collapse before they'd slink away, moaning, rejected. Meanwhile, I pounded away, trying to be fun, hunched furiously over the keyboard. No one said a word of encouragement. No one offered a drink. All I had were rapid-fire suggestions, demands, complaints, and then, like a tornado passing, everyone more-or-less gave up, and then they were gone. Suzanne left without saying goodbye.

A new event manager, kind of a dapper bear in a pink plaid shirt, appeared and signaled for me to stop with that kind of self-throat-slitting gesture—I was mid-song—because he wanted to move the piano and clean up the room. That's how it ended. In the sudden silence, the original planners came forward with the contracts and I signed some dotted lines. "I think that went well," one of them said.

"You do?" I asked.

"I think everyone had a great time."

"Really?"

Not wanting to argue, I kept quiet before nearly running out of the room.

Which brings me to this subway platform. My hands, my brain—everything's fried, but I don't feel an ounce of fulfillment. Only shame. Was it worth the $250?

A gig is a gig, as they say, so perhaps I'm being a bit dramatic. I, who always thought I could be a whore with no problem, but who just moments ago scrambled about the piano for my copy of "Chattanooga Choo-Choo" as a lifeline.

"That's good," whispered one of the planners in my right ear, gazing all the while at Suzanne as I oom-chump-chumped away. "Yes, 'Chattanooga Choo-Choo.'" My own eyes darted about the room wondering who was next and what they would want me to do.

"That's all we want," he purred. "Just something fun."

WANING PUBLIC INTEREST (A DIALOGUE)

Dear Adam,

My sincere apologies if I have kept you waiting, and as each day passes, I certainly don't want to keep you waiting any longer. Executive Director [name removed] and I have talked extensively about the realities of presenting a performance of Cage's seminal prepared piano works, and the only way we can surmise making this a viable endeavor is to partner with a higher education institution. We have reached out and made proposals to music faculty at [name removed] but have been unable to contract their support. As such, I regret to inform you that we have been unable to find a way to support the presentation of your concert in the fall. This is merely to be taken as a brute fact of the realities of artistic presentation in our day and age, and indicative of a waning public interest in contemporary classical music. We commend you for your artistic endeavors, and hope you stay in touch.

Dear [name removed]

Thanks for your response! It certainly is disappointing news, especially since we seemed to be so close to setting a date and budget before *[name removed]* left her position. She and I actually spoke over the phone and, without her ever mentioning *[name removed]* or any other partnerships, she seemed to have the utmost confidence in this performance happening with a simple and small budget.

But I understand. I've served as an arts presenter before and have experienced its myriad challenges. As for waning public interest in contemporary classical music, I can't really speak to this. Was the public consulted? I've played strictly modern programs to packed houses from Reno, Nevada to Juneau, Alaska. Several of my John Cage concerts this season have completely sold out, one of them half-a-year in advance. And I'm not famous.

Thank you for the consideration, and best of luck with the coming season!

FIGHT YOUR FEAR AND LOSE

The other day I received a large envelope in the mail from a competition I lost. Taken by surprise, I figured it might be some kind of certificate, maybe to make me feel better. Or perhaps, I thought for a second, my loss had all been a big misunderstanding and I'd actually WON! Yay! I won!

I opened the envelope in my kitchen and discovered that I had not, after all, won anything. But there was a conciliatory certificate saying I'd made it to the final round. How kind. Then I saw a sheet describing how the evaluators made their decisions and how I should consider their comments. Wait, what? Their comments? I flipped the sheet over and, to my terror, discovered another one behind it with my pieces listed— I'd submitted a full concert performance video—each with its own corresponding hand-written evaluation. Each evaluation had an opening summary of my playing.

I threw the packet on the table as if it was an evil thing and backed away. See, I live in a kind of happy lie where my playing is universally appreciated, my programming efforts understood, and my technique and interpretations admired. I also live simultaneously in the other extreme, where everything I do is bad, every compliment is a lie, and everyone knows full well that I'm a shabbily disguised impostor. The shaking of one belief or the confirmation of the other are both equally dreaded, dangerous, and potentially damaging. "I can't say anything to you without you getting upset," F often complains. Well, duh.

I had to leave my apartment to teach a lesson and, even though I wanted to, I didn't throw the evaluations away. Instead, I stuffed the packet into my tote bag to read on the subway platform. And what better place, really? Ten minutes later, I read the critiques and...well, nothing happened. I didn't fling myself before a 3 Train. I didn't crumble into a heap of tears. I didn't enter into an imaginary argument with the judges, defending my playing and pianistic philosophy. I didn't even curse myself for entering the competition in the first place. No, I didn't really have any reaction. The ideas I read about my phrasing and tone coloring seemed pretty reasonable, and I considered how I might incorporate the advice into future performances. That was it.

I particularly agreed with one point: My "repertoire was not ideal for evaluation." It's true. My program was all modern, mostly somber, often quiet, and heavy on the minimalism. Scriabin it was not, and intended to impress, never. After all, I submitted a video of a concert I had shaped for an *audience*, not a panel. And for the last five, maybe ten years, I've committed myself to making peace with the fact that when I play a concert, my motivation has nothing to do with impressing anybody. I keep entering these stupid competitions for any number of reasons, but when I lose them it reminds me of the pianist I am and the pianist I'm not—which together weirdly add up to the pianist I want to be. And this feels good, actually. Instead of some stranger, some assumed authority, granting me validation, I manage to produce—or I'm *forced* to produce—that validation myself. This is gratitude, and it might be the closest I ever come to winning anything.

A FUNNY THING HAPPENED ON THE WAY TO THE PIANO (or, HOW I LEARNED TO STOP WORRYING AND COME OUT OF THE CLOSET)

[*delievered at a Human Rights Campaign fundraiser in Boston*]

Before taking the stage at the Gund Gallery at Kenyon College, I listened as the gallery director introduced me with an impressive mash-up of my bio as it has appeared over the years. I stood on the sideline, humbled and blushing as she finally reached the conclusion: "Tendler will publish a memoir this winter about coming-out and coming-of-age during his America 88x50 tour." It occurred to me that these words, self-penned like most bios, had just confirmed my sexual identity to everyone in the room, whereas not too long ago my heart might have stopped at the idea of admitting even half as much to myself.

I've been "out" for about five years now, traversing a psychological landscape that has taken me from steadfast denial to, apparently, noting my sexuality in my bio. With such sudden openness shared between us in that gallery, my self-consciousness vanished—a rare thing. I stopped blushing at the *sound* of my bio, and in fact stood a little taller. After all, I'd fought for this openness (with myself mostly) for most of my life, and even the smallest reminder of that tattered past, that internal war, jolted me into a state of awareness and gratitude.

I looked out to the room, to the students especially, thinking about how I spent my college years closeted and celibate, by any measure antisocial and enmeshed in a dysfunctional relationship with the piano, a surrogate to which I assigned an impossible job—fix me

—and over which I created some illusion of having control and power. In turn, the piano often bit back. Even it needed a little space.

With ten years of professional transformation between those college days and my visit to Kenyon College as a visiting artist, representing a kind of professional example to the music students, some of whom wrote pieces expressly for me to play during my visit, it was still the relatively recent transformation from closet-case to "out" artist that made me, in hearing my bio right then, feel the most proud and accomplished.

Those in the audience at Kenyon who even caught the "coming-out" part of my introduction probably didn't care, and any of the more conservative souls in attendance might have just dismissed it as more gay yadda-yadda typical of our current cultural and political climate. But then, it's an election year [2012] and we in the gay community have once again found ourselves positioned as the targets, pawns, and ever-effective human leverage for cultural warfare.

We didn't ask for it. It's the opponents of gay rights (and safety, and health) really, who have kidnapped our private lives and dragged them into the courts, pinning them against public policy and putting us in the position of having to defend who we love in political and religious terms day after day lest we lose our rights to the pursuit of happiness and equal protection. Depending on the conflict, through the years we have had to become scientists, doctors, lawyers...

The other day I noticed a gay Facebook friend lamenting about "society," and how he hoped someday it would change so that he could come out to his co-workers and abandon the inconveniences of covering up his outside life. I watched as it all unfolded on his wall, as he countered the encouragement to come out with practiced, pragmatic explanations as to why he just "couldn't," his reasons mostly having to do with family and cultural expectations.

I get it. I've been there. And when one is in the closet, they typically believe the same story they tell everyone else. It's less "living a lie" and more believing your story. But the inconvenient thing about societies is that they don't actually change on their own. Rather, a society, a culture, is shaped by single people making single choices and, like an election, these small but crucial decisions add up. While every closeted person has their reasons to stay there, so has any person who has ever come out faced those same painful rationalizations and pushed forward. I would say it took me ten years to truly come to terms with the inevitability of coming out to my family, and I assure you that the good of society was the last thing on my mind.

Maybe part of the fun of gay life is that, with any luck, it always will feel a little against-the-grain, a jab at the status quo. Brunch becomes a protest. Sex, a riot. And maybe some people subconsciously choose to even stay hidden to retain that feeling of danger and adventure. Or maybe they don't want to call themselves "gay." I also get that, and myself would prefer open sexual fluidity in our culture, among men particularly, over strict labels. Fine. But lying—if you're actually lying to people, as I once was—gets old fast, and the hangover's a bitch. The euphoria of coming out dwarfs the thrill of sex in the closet in a New York minute.

I'll never forget breathing for the first time without a bowling ball in my chest, or noticing as my incurable colitis disappeared, or hearing my gay-sounding voice un-self-consciously for the first time, or realizing with some sorrow that the titillating feeling of danger and adventure I'd once maybe associated with being gay, and doing gay things, was probably not much more than some Darwinian by-product of…well, shame, a quietly building shame that began the very first time I realized I was what people would consider an "other," both dangerous and in danger if revealed. If outed. I began thinking this way, in terms of self-protection and strategy, before I even knew the specifics of what I was hiding. I don't think many people outside of our community can truly imagine the effect of living one day this way, let alone decades.

If there was a bigot in the crowd at the Gund Gallery for my performance, which I doubt, or more innocently, someone who graciously "tolerates" us gays and our so-called agenda, then they had to listen to me play the piano for an hour. They had to laugh with me in the Q&A. They had to become, in some ways, a friend, and in so doing might have gone from arms folded to arms outstretched. Harvey Milk, before his assassination, had aggressively urged gay people to come out and stay out as a political action, a societal service, because when anyone in the straight public knows just *one* of us, they will resist and diffuse the simplified stereotypes presented in pop culture and the fear tactics of power-hungry politicians and religious zealots.

Eventually tides will turn and enough public support will shift the balance toward non-discriminatory policies and unprejudiced social currents to emerge without the opposition we so typically endure today. Eventually, our fight for equality will go down as hallowed historical legend. People have died for these still-not-fully-realized rights and ideals, and the rest of us must remain vigilant not to fall on the wrong side of this fight's history.

So, societies don't change on their own, at least not for the better. It turns out that each one of us has a responsibility to create that change on our own, with patience, compassion, unity, and an iron fist. Existing in the first place helps.

PART THREE

CHILD

they surround him like a campfire. it's the second time this week i've seen him playing here in the caves below port authority. he plays well, or well enough, nuance and dynamics notwithstanding, with his strong, agile fingers out-performing any of the other child pianists i've seen on these subway platforms. but talent or not, music or mess, the spectacle always attracts a crowd, a fascinated, oddly supportive crowd, watching and filming as the child's stony-faced caretaker (should i put that word in quotation marks?) watches from the sidelines, almost hiding. money falls into the hat. homemade CDs shine under the lights. passers-by clap and disappear. no one winces at the piercing treble from a ruddy amplifier attached like a leash to the boy's keyboard. no one cringes at the tone clusters intermingled with mozart's "rondo alla turca" as it tumbles forward at breakneck speed. i keep my distance, quickening my pace, resenting (which is to say, admiring) the attention and adoration showered on the boy from his silent, transient circle of admirers, these strangers. and resenting his talent, too.

THERE WAS A FLY

I get a lot of thinking done at concerts. In fact, the amount of thinking I get done helps me to gauge afterwards how much I truly enjoyed the experience. Sitting in a concert is the closest thing I have to meditation.

I'm also terribly impatient, at least with fellow audience members, and much more compassionate onstage than off. Whereas onstage I don't quite care about what's going on out there in the hall, once I'm entrenched in the democracy of folding chairs and orchestra seating, any crinkling of a plastic bag, any whisper, any glance at a phone, will meet my deadly stare or a tap on the shoulder. I "shh" people, and once asked a girl sitting next to me to stop scrolling through photos on her digital camera during a friend's recital, an activity that, while rude, made no noise whatsoever. She was mortified. Good.

Tonight, the spellbinding pianist (and friend) Pedja Muzijevic had the floating concert hall, Bargemusic, which has never answered any of my emails, entranced. I was a puppy heeling before him, an eternal student in prostration. The composers' music flowed from his head to fingers like a waterfall, and he firmly channeled each piece's aural image without getting in its or his own way. He was pure. He was divine.

There was also a fly. Yes, it flew around his head in a continual, frenzied orbit. Even after a sizable intermission during which it seemed to vanish, it re-appeared just in time for the second half. This fly, giant in size, was a daredevil fly. An erratic fly, a provocative fly, zooming dangerously close to Pedja's face during some of the program's most demanding passages. In fact, Pedja seemed half-a-gasp away from swallowing this fly during Schumann's *Kreisleriana*. At least if that had happened we'd be rid of the thing.

There's no negotiating with a fly. We were, all of us, defenseless. This animal insisted on sharing the stage. Amidst my deep thinking about Pedja and his talent, his agile fingers, his elastic mind, and the weight of his program (which had me wondering if I'd played a proper recital in the last seven years) I wondered if this fly was necessary, a necessary reminder that we are all indeed tied to the here and now, even as the contrapuntal perfume of Schumann begs to sweep us away. Yes, there is a fly. There is always a fly.

Someone kicked over a soda can on the final chord of the slow, sixth movement of the Schumann. The waves of the East River caused the underbelly of Bargemusic to clank and groan. The people who still think that slow movements are a time to relax their manners uniformly coughed, whispered, and snacked.

But maybe these injustices tether us to reality and bring a crucial quality of urgency and risk (and madness) to the experience of live classical music. Perhaps it's the dissonance between our imperfect reality and the pursuit of perfection—and indeed both performer and audience do seek a kind of perfection from the experience—that fuels the excitement of a classical concert.

Every time I go to a recital I'm tantalized by the idea that my experience in that moment can't be *too* far off from a similar moment a century before, or last week, or the year my mom was born. But classical music is not just a time machine or museum piece. The people onstage are at work *right now*, activating a thing *right now*, and anything can happen *right now*. They know it and we know it. So tonight, I came face to face with Schumann, Scarlatti, Cowell, Feldman, and Liszt, and yet I also had the fortune of dipping briefly into Pedja's inner-world, a world that he could only be so bold and brave enough to share onstage. To live and die with each cadence—for me, this is classical music. Irrational, alive, buzzing.

PINOCCHIO

One of my older students uses a piano instruction book from 1956. It has markings in it from every period of his life, and the book itself serves as a kind of time capsule, with almost every page offering some dizzying finger exercise or cluttered attempt at teaching a key signature. Of the eighty-five little pieces, several serve as politically incorrect postcards from early twentieth century America, with songs like "In Old Japan" and "The Jolly Tar." I personally like "The Laughing Fairy." My student started working on the final piece, called "Italian Dance," about a month ago.

This book, which he has owned for nearly half-a-century, is falling apart, and the last page probably went missing before I was born. "Italian Dance," hence, had no ending when we started it. In fact, we only could experience a measure of the Coda before having to quit.

I love scooping up old, out-of-print piano books, so I pounced on the opportunity to track this one down. For one, I thought it actually had some good music in it, and second, we would finally find out how "Italian Dance" ended. I found it online, bought it for $20 (the printed price on the actual book is $3.25) and have forgotten to bring it to our lessons ever since. I've peeked inside and there are only two lines of music that follow where we've had to stop, but for three lessons now the poor guy has asked if I remembered to bring the book, and I've had to tell him each time that I forgot.

So today, as per usual, we played through it and stopped at the first measure of the Coda. He likes to stay focused in our lessons, indulging in very little side conversation, but I had to say something. I told him that our relationship with "Italian Dance" reminded me of my childhood.

My father and mother divorced when I was two, I explained, but my father still visited rather frequently, if irregularly, and often on weekends. With him, he would sometimes bring stacks of VHS tapes filled to capacity with dubbed movies. I don't know if anyone besides me remembers how to do this, but one could basically wire two VCRs together and then record one VHS tape to another. You could also do this with a home camcorder. Anyway, one could also select the quality of the recording, standard play or extended play, two hours of blank tape versus six hours. Choosing quantity over quality, my dad would dub the movies in extended play and pack three movies to a tape. Or, I should say, almost three.

So I'd get this succession of films on one tape, always totally mismatched—*The Goonies* followed by *Scanners* followed by *Return to Oz*—but of course movies have different lengths, and three movies will rarely fit evenly onto one tape, even in extended play. Thus, sometimes the ending of the third movie would get cut off.

Such was the case with *Pinocchio*. I fucking loved *Pinocchio*. I watched it more than any other Disney film, but the ending, because of the movie's third position on the dubbed tape, was cut off. I mean, right at the pivotal moment where the whale barreled toward *Pinocchio* for his final attack, just then, the tape would stop and begin automatically rewinding. Every time I'd wonder if the tape might magically go a tiny bit further, or actually somehow produce the end of the movie. But I never saw what happened next, what happened to the whale nor to Pinocchio. I had *heard* that he turned into a real boy, but never actually saw it.

That is, until one day when I finally rented it at a local video store so I could see for myself. I still remember the thrill of going past that expected cut-off point, seeing the whale suddenly coming straight toward the screen, mouth open. I'd never seen that before. And I still remember the sweet despair of seeing Pinocchio lying facedown in the tidepools, and the awe I felt when he woke up transformed, his face smooth and human, a real boy.

ON REALIZING DREAMS COME TRUE

A little less than twenty years ago, I got my first real gig. It was playing services at a little white Methodist church in the neighboring village of Williamstown, Vermont. Like most church gigs, I had to prepare some preambulum and postlude music, as well as a number of assigned hymns. The pay was $40 for the hour. Not bad for a twelve-year-old. I practiced for these services all week, terribly nervous. It was the first time there were stakes in my playing. My mom, hearing flubbed chords and wrong notes, would remind me about the seriousness of my new role. "You can't make any mistakes on Sunday," she would say. "This isn't like your lessons."

All in all, the gig lasted about a month, and though I don't remember any real disasters, there were definitely shaky rhythms, unintended dissonances and false starts. I was, after all, learning the ropes. I distinctly remember one time, maybe my last time, when the minister sprang a new hymn on me mid-service. I froze. I didn't know what to do. My piano teacher, who got me the gig in the first place and who (astonishingly) came to each service I played, swooped in to the rescue. Maybe he came for exactly this reason, to help in the event of an emergency. He sat at the upright and played the hymn without hesitation as the congregation sang along. It was perfect. How did he do that? He played it better at first glance than I could if I'd had all week.

On the drive home, pouting, I said to my mom from the passenger seat in disbelief, "I can't believe he could just play it like it was nothing."

"He's been playing piano for a long time, Adam," she said with the tender yet unbudging tone she'd no doubt learned to adopt whenever I sank into one of my self-deprecating funks.

"I wish I could sight-read a hymn like that."

"Well," she said, "someday you will."

BLESSED

I waited about ten minutes while one of my older students, a woman in her sixties, finished up a phone call with her rabbi. From the sounds of it, she was planning a bar mitzvah, arranging everything from the start time to the cake design to the seating. "I want it to be a nice," she urged. "People should feel like it's special." Between breaths, she whispered apologies in my direction. I waved it off. This sounded important. At last she hung up and came to the piano. "It's a lot of work!" she said, regarding the shih tzu on the floor, "getting Muffin blessed."

POST-PERFORMANCE DEPRESSION (CRYING IN MALIBU)

When I first set up my social media platforms, I told myself that I would aim to present my experience as a classical musician as honestly as possible, even if it meant not always looking cool. Even before I was kept abreast of my colleagues' activities on social media, they always seemed to have cool stuff going on—gigs, residencies, grants, commissions—and I typically greeted their good news with a three-part mix of joy, despair, and skepticism. Meanwhile, I was mopping floors in a West Village gay bar, substitute teaching in inner-city schools, and stealing practice time whenever I could for concerts that didn't exist yet. No, I didn't feel cool. When people first read my blog they thought I was suicidal.

Far from it, I was fueled, like any artist, by a kind

of tenacity tangled in doubt but rooted in a core of confidence. That kernel of confidence, which no one really wants to admit having, is the only reason why any of us stay in the game. Over the past few years, I've figured out how to connect some of the dots (also, to see them in the first place), and have begun to trust that I *do* have a life in music, but that there is very little in it which I control. I do, however, feel like I have a responsibility to honor it with work. Constant work. Obsessive work.

It's part of why I shake my head no when people ask if I crash after a big concert. "Of course not!" I say, because I almost always have something new lined up to occupy my attention. But as I trudge through this month, helplessly observing a half-present version of myself struggling through conversations and daily tasks, lashing out and self-flagellating in continuous rotation, avoiding friends, phone calls and social gatherings, I have to own up to the fact that this is all happening on the heels of an exhilarating performance I gave last month in Brooklyn, and that this has all happened before. Maybe I suffer from post-performance depression, after all.

Last year around this time, I'd just performed at the Rubin Museum. The performance, presented by WQXR, sold out completely. I also played well. Nearly a year of preparation and anticipation led up to the event, and I hobbled through the weeks that followed it in a fog. I'd even lined up another performance, an ambitious, multimedia "reading recital," but found myself immobilized by a kind of grief, wandering the apartment, barely practicing. Every idle moment felt like a betrayal of my potential, a squandering of my future, and worst of all, proof that I wasn't cut from the same cloth as my still very cool colleagues. The day before the recital, while numbly washing dishes and staring into space, hating myself after wasting precious time that morning drooling in front of my computer screen, a glass shattered in my hand. I'll always have a scar where a chunk of my knuckle went missing.

Years earlier, when I finished my fifty state America 88x50 tour, I languished for a summer in Malibu, working at a veterinary clinic while figuring out what to do next. I still remember staring out at the sea and crying. I was 24, living in Malibu, and had just received an offer to direct a new music nonprofit in Houston starting in the fall. Truth be told, I had nothing to cry about.

I've tried churches, support groups, emotional affairs, journaling, therapy, The Artist's Way, exercise, new age spiritual reprogramming seminars, all in an attempt to avoid, as one self-help book put it, "intolerable reality," to help unblock my creativity, maximize my efficiency, and keep my mood coasting at a healthy equilibrium. But what happens is, eventually some commitment sweeps in and saves the day as I rise to its challenge. This starting-over fills the void, often excruciatingly so, and I begin again.

A musician treats their career like a garden. We plant seeds and hope they grow. The best of us never stop planting, watering, and tending, and ideally, one stretch of concerts will arc as another few breach the soil. Ideally.

I looked pretty cool last year, with concerts every month in different boroughs and time zones. I'd arrived, so it appeared—so I made it appear, now on social media myself—and still I hustled throughout, trying to line up things for the future. My activities climaxed, I suppose, last month with that concert in Brooklyn, but right now my garden looks a little sad. An older student just asked what I had coming up, and before I could explain, let alone finish saying the words "I don't know," he interrupted me with, "What?!"

I live in New York with a loving (and forgiving) partner. I'm publishing a book that I've spent seven years developing. I've begun gnawing into a new program on a beautiful grand piano that I recently bought. I'm paying my bills with music—an incredible feat—and, yes, I've accepted invitations to play here and there. I have no reason to panic, to have these dark, sleepless circles under my eyes, to shrug when people ask how I'm doing. But still, I'm crying in Malibu.

I suppose it's only natural to feel vulnerable in these resetting moments, learning new music, cold-calling presenters, feeling like a beginner in every way. The laboratory is a lonely place. In the thick of practice and the daily grind of proposing concerts, one has only their faith to keep the engine running. A musician in this purgatory is a runner at high-altitude, functioning fine enough but also intensely aware of the difference between that present moment and their ideal atmosphere. We suffer privately, and in the meantime every "yes" feels like redemption and every "no thanks" like a doomed fate confirmed.

Of course I'm projecting, but I think any musician might agree, the hustle, the build, the high, the crash, the starting over, it might all be part of the artistic experience that keeps us hooked. It's a Jacob's Ladder of a process, sure, and a remarkable fact that we musicians will trade in hours, days, weeks, or years of ours lives for a few moments of, not fame or recognition, but pure connection, connection with an audience, a composer, ourselves. Then it's over, like a novel scrawled on a blackboard, read aloud imperfectly, and then erased.

Yes, we may all look very cool via our avatars, but I think classical musicians also develop a distinct kind of humility from our vocations. Cliché as it might sound, we stand before a new project as one stands before a mountain, and learn to embrace every doubt-soaked minute until we actually share the work as being part of the miracle—the miracle of our lives in music, the garden we grow, and the trust we share with whomever listens. We have perhaps more interest in the view on the way up than the summit itself. What summit? We climb, and keep climbing, functioning best at high altitude.

PART FOUR

HOLOCAUST

It's a distinctly gay phenomenon to open a first edition book by Edmund White from 1982, see an inscription inside from one friend to another, and wonder nonchalantly if either one of them is still alive.

UNTITLED

I was sitting on a bench in Central Park one day when my mom called me in tears. "I'm so sorry to do this," she cried, "but I have to tell you what I just saw." She described coming upon some stopped cars on our road, near where the pavement turns to dirt, and people standing in a circle. "So I stopped the car, too. I thought maybe there was an accident or something."

But instead, she saw that the group—men, woman, children—all surrounded a deer lying on the shoulder of the road, struck by a truck. "It was still alive, though," she said through her tears. "Then the man who hit it went back to his truck and...you know, I thought he might call the game warden or something—but no, he brought out a gun."

I hadn't heard my mother cry in about a year, and

the sound paralyzed my body, left me immobilized. It always does. I felt my own chest begin to tickle and grow heavy, like I might cry, too. But I stayed silent and listened. "He walked over to the deer and raised the rifle on his shoulders and..." She didn't need to finish the sentence. She gulped, sobbed, sniffled. "And you know the worst part? The people standing around, they didn't even look away or cover their eyes. They just watched and plugged their ears."

ON HURTING PEOPLE, OR ANOTHER VERSION OF HOW I CAME OUT

My last relationship before coming out was with someone I met over Craigslist. It was summer of 2006, and I'd just completed the America 88x50 tour. I was watching my sister's apartment in Malibu for the summer, working at a veterinary clinic, and Craigslist seemed like the safest place for hooking up. He and I met for lunch after exchanging a couple pictures and chatting over Yahoo Messenger (another closet go-to for me in the early-to-mid 2000s) and it turned out we actually liked each other. We starting dating, if you could call it that, for my remaining time in California before moving to Texas. So about a month.

Still, throughout our sex on the beach (better in theory), dinner dates, movies, phone calls and short dips into each other's non-closet worlds (more mine than his; he met my sister, for instance), I never actually had *his* phone number. When he called me, UNAVAILABLE flashed across the cell phone screen. I met him thinking his name was Jason. Later, he told me it was John.

When I left California, we sort of said we'd keep in touch. Everything with him was sort of. And I felt embarrassed even admitting to myself that I would actually miss him, something he never expressed toward me, and thus something I'm sure I never quite confessed out loud.

But we did keep in touch. While I found my footing in Texas, he kept me updated on his ever-changing email addresses and Yahoo screen names. And when I visited LA again that year, we met up and I even almost spent the night. Almost. Sort of. When I told him about how I would make my Houston debut at the Rothko Chapel that spring playing John Cage, he said he would come. I thought he was joking until a week or so before the performance when he sent me his flight information. I told him I wasn't sure how I could pick him up and shuttle him around, but he assured me that he liked trying out public transportation in new cities, and not to worry.

We still had known each other less than a year and still only sporadically communicated, but it appeared I would be hosting him before the week's end. After some fancy footwork, I had my sister and mother, who would visit for the performance, staying in a hotel, and John, who I described to them as a "visiting friend," staying with me.

He did come to Houston. He did come to the concert. But he didn't stay with me. Instead, he booked himself into a bed and breakfast a few blocks away from my apartment in the Montrose, Houston's sultry gay ghetto, thick with trees that help conceal its restaurants and bars, themselves mostly converted houses and garages.

After my performance, he almost stayed over, but retreated in the wee hours to his rented room. The next day, he explored Houston as I went on a trip to Galveston with my sister and mother. I was miserable and they couldn't understand why. Nor could I, really. I'd just had a successful concert. They were visiting. I had a "friend" in town. What was the problem? I couldn't tell them the truth, which I could barely bring myself to comprehend: I was finally, undeniably, living a double life, and this is precisely when, through the years, I'd told myself I would come out.

I moved to Houston with the personal resolve to no longer lie about my sexuality. That is, to at least no longer tell people I was straight if the subject came up. Still, I wasn't necessarily ready to tell them I was gay. I simply planned to evade the subject more vaguely than before. But I always told myself that once I started really, truly lying *to my family*, no longer just hooking up but rather conducting deeper and more meaningful affairs, that's when I would pull the trigger. And here it was.

Later that night, John and I went to a now-closed Greek pizza place in Montrose called Biba's, and I told him about the crossroads at which I'd arrived. It didn't go well. "I don't need to *label* myself to feel better about myself," he said. "It's not such a big deal to me."

"But you would never tell your family about me," I argued back, "and there's a reason for that. So it *is* a big deal to you."

On and on this went. Me arguing my point, and him saying I was pressuring him to categorize his sexuality.

"But is this working for you?" I asked. "This secret life? Because it's not for me. Not anymore."

It was the first time I'd said such a thing out loud

to another person. But I didn't feel freed or relieved. What I felt in that moment, most of all, was hurt. This guy, this John, would rather conduct our relationship behind closed doors than entertain the idea of joining me in the open. It felt like a personal affront, like I didn't mean enough to him.

"I just flew across the country to see you," he said. "And you want more evidence?"

We didn't even try to spend that night together. He went back to his room and I returned to my apartment. My sister and mother, banished to their hotel, had no idea a war was being waged in Montrose, the gayborhood where I, of course, had chosen to live.

The next day, John and I awkwardly roamed the city's parks and attractions. I remember we even wandered into a realtor's open house. I barely said a word, still infuriated about how he couldn't appreciate what had taken me years to understand myself. He called it a need to label ourselves, and I called it a need to stop living a very tired and tiring masquerade. There was a difference. He couldn't see it, but finally I could. He left that afternoon on an earlier flight than he'd originally booked, and a couple weeks later I came out.

John and I exchanged a couple of polite emails. I apologized in one of them for my behavior that weekend. Once, he even sent a letter. And then silence. About half a year went by before he called. It was around Christmas, and we talked as I drove my car down a decorated Kirby Drive in Houston's wealthier shopping district. When I told him that I now had a boyfriend who would join me in Vermont for the holidays, he fell silent for a nearly imperceptible moment, a moment frozen in my memory, because after we hung up a few minutes later, he vanished from my life compeltely. Emails bounced, and I'd lost the letter he sent, so I didn't have an address. I couldn't find him anywhere on the Internet, and wondered if I was searching for him using what had perhaps always been a fake name. John? Jason?

I was puzzled. I mean, *had* we been dating? Were we exclusive? Did this person with whom I had such critical differences still think of me in some way as his companion? How could I have missed that? Perhaps just as I'd failed to see the depth of his gesture when he'd visited Texas, maybe I'd also assumed too little about our relationship after that rocky but revealing weekend.

Another little part of me actually felt as if, in coming out, I'd somehow failed or betrayed him. He was strong enough to stay in the closet, so I told myself, and the closet had been our bond of sorts, and here I'd gone ahead and "labeled myself" and was doing big gay things like having a boyfriend and bringing him home for Christmas. Perhaps the closet always retains a kind of irrational, exotic appeal, and I realized in my new gay glory that it never quite loses its contagious power. For a minute, I felt guilty enough to wish I'd stayed there. For him. And my ego.

But he was gone. Nothing on Google, and nothing on Facbeook years later once I joined and found myself still searching every couple of months. Whenever visiting LA, I'd peer into passing cars looking for his face.

Then, two winters ago, while taking the PATH train home from a teaching gig in New Jersey, I saw him. I couldn't believe my eyes. He was seated and talking to a professor-looking guy on the opposite end of the train. I paced, I circled, and of course thought about how fucking weird it was to discover my California boyfriend, who for years I'd searched for, on a PATH train in New Jersey.

Finally, I interrupted their conversation and said hello. John stared blankly up from his seat, as if he didn't recognize me, and managed only to offer a few foggy cordialities, nodding his head and squinting his eyes as if he was trying, or pretending, to remember. "Well, good to see you," I finally said, exhausted and resisting the urge to shake him, to remind him that he'd once, only a few years earlier, bought a plane ticket to visit me in the Lone Star State—his first and, I can assume, only time there. *Do you remember going to Texas?* I wanted to scream. But I didn't. I didn't even say his name, still wondering if I had the real one. After all, I wouldn't want to embarrass him in front of his friend.

We both got off at the Journal Square platform, where I needed to transfer, and I saw John and the professor part ways. Then he came over to talk to me. He still acted as if the memory of us was too distant to verily recall. He didn't remember my name? He didn't remember dating a concert pianist? He didn't stalk me online like I did him? "You visited me in Texas," I said bluntly. "You saw me play John Cage at the Rothko Chapel in Houston. You can't tell me you don't remember that."

"Yeah..." he said, still dazed. "Well, we should get together. Do you have, uh... you know, a boyf—...a boyfr..." he stuttered over the word.

"Yeah, I do," I said. He nodded, looking a little sad. And again, I felt embarrassed.

"Well, let's grab lunch sometime," he said.

"Absolutely. What's your number?"

He squirmed. "How about you give me yours."

"Really?" I said. "Really?"

I acquiesced and watched him enter my number into a flip phone. I thought a couple things: that either he hadn't changed and was still in the closet, or that he was protecting himself from me because once upon a time, I'd really hurt him. He closed his phone, and we said goodbye, and I knew I would never hear from him again. It's sad. I would have really liked to catch up.

THE CIRCUMCISION OF DAVID

In college, a friend visited my apartment and saw a framed picture that my sister gave me for Christmas of a doctor superimposed over an image of Michelangelo's David statue, swabbing and operating on the statue's member. I later found out that he spread a titillating rumor around the music school that I had pictures of naked guys hanging all over my apartment. People often ask me why it took so long to come out.

NEW YORK

a girl on the 1 train dribbles coffee on herself while taking a sip from her thermos, laughs in disbelief and says to the woman sitting across the aisle, "i fuckin' hate this city."

LATIN LESSON

i just looked up the expression "persona non grata" to see if it could in any way apply to how the piano faculty at IU has treated me since i graduated, and it turns out to be exactly the perfect definition.

BREVARD

I only remember one person from the two weeks I spent at Brevard Music Center, a blur of days when I escaped often, walking to town on a long strip of blacktop just to get away, and then finally packed my things and left without saying goodbye, not even to him. I don't remember his name, but he was a big guy with blonde hair and a southern accent. Arkansas, I now remember. A trumpet jock, he and I would pal around, and I attached myself to him like I had many a trumpet jock before and after. One night while I practiced he kind of wandered into my room and asked if I would show him how fast I could play. "Play the fastest thing you can," he demanded. Of course I refused. "Please," he continued. "Don't be weird. I just want to see." This went on for a while, him pleading for me to play fast and me saying no.

Now, if you know a trumpeter, imagine asking

them, out of the blue, to play their highest note for you. They'd probably tell you to go fuck yourself.

Anyway, I finally surrendered and played a chromatic scale up and down an octave as fast as I could. "Come on, you can play faster than that," he said. I tried again. "No really, go faster." And it probably wasn't long after that that I left.

FALL

    tonight, brushing my teeth, i laughed thinking about the time i spent an evening with a prominent new music ensemble after their concert, and how i'd wanted to impress them and look my best, and how at the end of the night i scurried into the middle of ninth avenue to hail them a cab, tripped, flew forward and landed flat on the pavement, scraping my hands as they screamed.

CLOSET THOUGHT

(subway platform, 110th and Central Part West)

People speak of the closet like it's some planet with a surface you can inhabit. But really it's more like Jupiter, or one of those planets they say is made of gas, huge and suffocating, but less there than actually there. I never understood those planets, how they exist, what they even mean. A planet like that, could you just fly right through it? I look back on my years in the closet with the same curious fascination, as if regarding some astral body from afar. What was that place, void of gravity and oxygen? How could life survive? Was there ground to stand on, or do you just fly right through it?

IN DEFENSE OF THE CLUSTER

Over half a century ago, John Cage ushered in the last great dissonance: silence. Audiences and performers, far from making peace with the idea of clearing a spot at the table for "nothing," still wriggle and camp their way though pieces like 4'33", convinced that surely they must do something to fill the void, unnerved by the opportunity to let time, air and space do its thing, and consoled only by making the silence 'about' them. A performer ridiculously dramatizes the piece by sighing, perhaps, or an audience member ridiculously pulls out their own stopwatch and gawks at it, another intentionally squeaks their chair.

But besides silence, I would argue that we still have another aural line in the sand, one introduced most sensationally by Henry Cowell in the early twentieth century. The cluster. I should clarify, I'm talking about the chromatic tone cluster, with black and white notes all smushed together at the same time.

The first time I encountered a cluster, it was in a Bastien kids piano book called *Dinosaur Kingdom*, a movement called "Brontosaurus." I crossed out the example of how to play the cluster with a dozen slashes of red ink, apparently not a fan.

Nowadays, clusters are hardly at their zenith of novelty in modern music, but I think that they, and silence, still both get under people's skin for the same reason. A story: The other day, a ten year old student walked in on me practicing music by Luciano Berio. The clusters stood out as something totally new to his eyes and ears; he'd never seen anyone intentionally play the piano this way. When I showed him the notation and technique for playing the clusters, he innocently and not-at-all disparagingly observed, "That's something a baby could do." Defensively, I demanded an explanation, and he replied that all he meant was that a cluster, in essence, is the most basic action of piano playing, perhaps the *first* possible action of piano playing. Indeed, a toddler would much rather place a palm into the keyboard than isolate a finger and press a single key. My student had a point; babies and cats and items we drop onto the keyboard all produce clusters. Inelegant clusters, but clusters all the same.

It's a chord with only a flash of an identity, defined by borders: top note, bottom note, with everything in between. Clusters can sound like the sludgy brownish-black that results when kids try to paint but end up mixing the colors all together, or tonefully melodic, as Cowell was reported to have played them, or at lightning speed they can come across as pure, tone*less* energy, lightning, like Scriabin's trills.

F has learned to cope with a lot regarding my

practicing. He has heard everything from pointillism to minimalism, but the only time this patient Italian has shouted "basta!" lately has been when I've practiced the cluster passages of these Berio pieces. Why? Well, perhaps because as precisely as Berio chooses to notate his clusters, and as clean and un-clustery as they might (or should theoretically) sound, when you put a ton of them all over the place in a polyrhythmic clusterfuck, the result is a provocative harkening back to what my student alluded to, a whiff of the primitive, a postcard from our collective pianistic infancy when all we knew how to do was splash our hands across the piano. It's psychologically (and physically) humbling for a performer to dive into clusters, these things that should be easy to play but aren't, and for the listener who doesn't see the meticulous score or understand the difficulty in producing a well-executed cluster... well, it can all sound a little insane. And shocking. And offensive. Or funny.

Even in 2014. Cowell's two-armed battlefield of clusters, *Antimony* from 1917, is still probably one of the most outrageously shocking pieces of music I've put before an audience.

But even amongst performers and composers, the cluster can look like a non-choice or a cop-out—"just a cluster"—not a complicated chord whose voicing a composer labored over, that a pianist had to practice to get into their fingers. The cluster remains contentious, daring us to dismiss it. It's the anarchy chord. The all-of-the-above chord. And it still has power to disrupt and disturb. Like Cage's silences, the cluster strings a tightrope through the subconscious realm of "anyone could do it" and in doing so, splinters the artifice that classical music is the work and realm of the gifted few, of the blessed geniuses. Instead of nothing, it invites *everything* to the table. The grown-ups stir and force a smile. Kids love it.

LOADING THE WOODSTOVE

i'm remembering the winter night, over ten years ago, when he visited for the first time in years, emerging from the trees in the dark early evening on a snowmobile, pulling it in front of the house and i thought, 'my hero,' and i thought, 'who travels by snowmobile?' and i thought, 'how did he do it?' and i thought, 'god, i spent years trying to lose this asshole,' and i thought 'he still looks great,' and i thought 'he still smells like how he smells, and smiles like how he smiles, and talks like how he talks.'

our night was calm and understated, built around nothing more than talking about what had happened in the years since high school when we'd gone our separate ways—very separate ways—while eating pizza, drinking beer and watching television. when my family went to sleep and we remained in the basement, tv on, woodstove roaring, he shrugged when i asked if he would stay the night. i kept feeding the fire to keep the basement warm. i don't remember how it started, but it ended with sobs and convulsions and the release of so many years' worth of anger and love and pain and lies and whatever emotion we feel when we miss someone and can't tell them, from one into the other, and like a puzzle i still remember how we fit. then silence, and then separate ways again. very separate ways. but i still think of that night whenever i'm home and it's winter and i'm loading the woodstove.

ANYONE ELSE

      my favorite art isn't the kind that makes me think that no one else could have made it and thus it's a work of genius (intimidation), but rather that which makes me think anyone else could've made it and thus it's a work of genius (inspiration).

GROW UP

the more i grow up, the less i'm able to tolerate charles ives's puritanical bullshit. and it's too bad, because it was ives's music that, as a teenager, first invited me to the modern music ball when i scarcely knew what modern music was. and it's too bad, because as an undergrad in music school i fought tooth and nail for special-admittance to a graduate level course on ives's music, studying and writing about it in-depth under the guidance of one of the world's foremost ives scholars. and it's too bad, because i went on to perform and speak about ives's music in all fifty states, telling his story with the same myth and pathos that had first enchanted and carried me through nearly a decade of autumn-tinged ives fantasia.

but now? as in right now, this moment, today, as

i read (for the who-knows-how-manyieth time) the rather famed letter ives's wife wrote to the wife of composer carl ruggles about their mutual friend, composer henry cowell—cowell, who was ives's first (and at first, only) ally, and who at the time was locked up in a 4-foot san quentin jail cell for his crimes of homosexuality involving a couple of seventeen year olds who went to the cops in retaliation when cowell said they couldn't borrow his car (really)—the picture she paints for mrs. ruggles of ives is not of the mysterious and tragic grandfather of american music, but rather that of a couch-fainting drama queen, naive to the point of absurdity, throwing a temper tantrum while turning a blind eye to the numerous faggots to whom he solely owed his reputation as a composer. bitch, please. grow up.

    i should be well used to this story by now, and i thought i was, but today it just doesn't fit. not for me, not anymore. nor does the story really feel "of the time" or any of that other nonsense. i can no longer make excuses for ives's lame-brain, str8-acting fanaticism. and for me it has finally begun to drag down his music.

and it's too bad, because suddenly that music's gnarliness doesn't strike me as audacious, but rather as annoying, and its sweetness, which once knotted my stomach and quivered my cheeks, comes across as the irritating nostalgia of a very rich man fetishizing a very imaginary postcard.

oh, danbury...

have you *been* to danbury?

i used to weep for ives, but today it seems so foolish, so mistaken and misplaced. but then, there's always tomorrow. maybe i can once again forgive. i guess, like so many of the pianists who have championed his music, i was in the closet once, too.

SOME CALL IT HISTORY

whatever it is we share

renders me speechless, thoughtless

emptied of character and definition

and anything i once liked about myself

or you

PART FIVE

SPRING

the melting, smoky smell of spring. coming out of a funk, i guess. i don't know. i want to quit all the time and feel more fake than ever. so fake i can barely begin or finish any sentences, and when i do my stomach hurts.

GOING UP

in the house where i grew up, we had a half-bath downstairs. it was a no frills affair, this bathroom, but as a kid i would enter it and shut the door, and it would turn into an elevator, taking me upstairs. no one else knew it was an elevator. i never opened the door to see the upstairs kitchen and shag-carpeted living room waiting behind it. i didn't need to. i'd just wait there a bit, leering at the magical crack between the floor and the doorframe, certain i had seen a shift from downstairs to upstairs. and then, when the time was right, i would will the elevator to go back down, opening the door and exiting the same way i entered, only now giddy and warm with the secret knowledge that i'd gone up, then come back down. no one else knew it was an elevator.

DO YOU DO

in philadelphia during a rehearsal, a pianist from curtis asked me what i do. "this," i said, motioning around to the other pianos in the room. a little later, the same person pointed to another pianist who would play in the same concert as us, a pioneer and recognized leader in our field, and he asked, "so what's *he* do?" puzzled, i again answered and gestured toward the piano. "*this*. this is what he does." so i guess i have a question, too. what are they teaching pianists at curtis?

APPLAUSE SHAME

I'll probably never forget how it felt when, a couple months ago in Philadelphia, I pressed the final two simultaneous notes of Morton Feldman's *Palais de Mari* and one of them didn't sound. I had feared this would happen, and by the time I reached that final measure it seemed that my heart pounded louder than the music—not an unreasonable possibility with Feldman. It all came down, in my mind, to those two perfect tones, two tones that indeed I had already played in an earlier passage and thought: "See? You just played them, and played them perfectly, so that means you can play them again. Don't you dare psych yourself out three minutes from now."

But then it happened. Of course it happened. I failed to play two soft notes at the same time, something any toddler could do in their first piano lesson. Faced with this, I couldn't, you know… try again, effectively composing a new ending to this classic work by Morton Feldman. No. I couldn't do anything. I just counted the beats until the measure terminated. And then the worst part.

They began clapping. Yes, the whole room applauded. Some stood. I wanted to run straight down the aisle and out the door. Either that or start over. At the very least, I wanted to explain, to apologize. In any event, I didn't want to bow. But I did. And I did again. And I accepted warm words of praise from those generous people, including Feldman's niece.

It was a long train ride back to New York, and I didn't spare a single person who asked how it went from the story of those last two notes. Eventually I moved past despair to practical considerations, how I could prevent the same thing from happening next time. Next time.

Always next time. Oh, how I prayed for a next time.

But you know, this happens to a certain extent after every performance. I locate an unforgivable offense, usually one that trumps a series of others, and then really dig into it, its origins, its implications, and all the reasons why it would never, ever conceivably happen to another pianist. Guilt, regret, shame. "It must be exhausting," a friend once said to me. I'd never really thought about it.

People in the audience wept during a concert I played a couple nights ago [Nathan Hall's *Tame Your Man*, for bondage artist and pianist, at the New Music Gathering at Peabody Conservatory]. Thousands have watched the video and hundreds have weighed in with comments, though undoubtedly this is because I worked alongside a brilliant musician and intellectual who also happens to be an adult film star. Still, I can't bring myself to watch the concert nor peruse the comments, even though the ones I've glimpsed have glowed with moving testimonies. No, I still fear the discovery of someone who will call me out on a missed note or sloppy passage. Because I know I can do better. I *wish* I could do bett—

"You're a textbook control freak," said a composer friend a couple months ago. I didn't expect it, but his "reading" gave context to what until then had just felt like plain old routine anguish. If I couldn't control others' perceptions of my work—and none of us can—I'd stew on it, avoid it, deflect it (especially if it was good), or try to beat them to the critical punch.

The performer inside me who emerges onstage is rapturous, selfless, primal and unapologetic, but also unpredictable. When a piece ends and the applause starts, that performer disappears and the control freak sweeps in to assess the damage, eager to promise better behavior next time while excusing the mess.

Maybe I'm apologizing for apologizing. But maybe, in identifying this twitch, I can transcend a behavior that I fall back on, depend on, rely on, but that doesn't serve me in any productive way. Isn't that what most of us would call a habit?

KNOW WHAT

burned, frozen

I don't know what

but those cords

we used to talk

through

or on, they're

burned, frozen

I don't know what

THANK YOUR HECKLERS

All music is new music to somebody. The other day, a friend messaged me that her students' eyes "nearly popped out when they saw all the screws in the piano" as she taught about John Cage's prepared piano works. It reminded me that, yes, people out there still hadn't actually heard of the prepared piano, just as I hadn't heard of it until one day as a teenager when I stumbled upon a dusty LP in my high school library. These first-encounters happen every day.

I still find myself surprised by even centuries-old repertoire. My jaw hit the floor last month when I saw Anthony Newman perform a Bach organ work unfamiliar to me that employed only the pedals for what seemed like an eternity. Revolutionary, I thought. And yet, he'd probably known of, or even played, the piece since he was a kid.

Last Saturday I played a concert of John Cage's music at the New York Public Library for the Performing Arts in Lincoln Center. Going into it, I felt a little insecure about the program, mostly tranquil works interspersed with readings. These are the hits, I thought. Well, two things happened: 1) Some people really loved the program, and had possibly never heard anything quite like it before. Wow. 2) Some people really hated the program, and had possibly never heard anything quite like it before. Wow.

I'd share the messages people sent since Saturday about how the concert touched their hearts and opened their minds to the breadth of Cage's music and writing, but of course I'm drawn more to the small faction of folks who created a disturbance throughout the performance. Hecklers, so I called them.

"Why don't you shut up!" one person groaned as

I answered a question asked by the curator of the series during an onstage interview. "Look at him, he looks more miserable than I am!" another remarked during a particular moment of concentration. "What do you want!" echoed through the hall during one of the more serene moments of the program, perhaps in response to someone else asking this person to be quiet. "This is ridiculous," another person announced as I performed Cage's *Radio Music* (1956) before the concert even started, as the audience took their seats.

These were all "unusually overt distractions," as one friend texted me later, and indeed I have my doubts that the interruptions came from individuals we'd describe as mentally stable—this was, after all, a free afternoon concert, and audiences for these affairs can be a mixed bag—yet the chaos both helped make the afternoon, shall we say, *memorable*, and reminded me that even what seemed like the most harmless of programs could still have the power to shake and provoke.

The composer Gerald Busby, who attended, wrote in an email: "You use the word hecklers, but I think those that made intrusive noises were actually just reacting to the beauty and terror of being present. They weren't heckling you; they were heckling the intimate precariousness of being awake and alive if only for a few seconds."

The intimate precariousness of being awake and alive... I often forget that we in the music community have the sacred opportunity to open a path toward absolute presence for our listeners, whether they embrace or reject it. Or even notice. We remember those moments of first discovery in our musical upbringings—and let's hope we're still open to such discoveries in adulthood—but now we have become the *ambassadors* of such moments. Is it really just a job? It can feel like a blessing.

I remember the first time I heard Copland's *Piano Variations*. I didn't know what to do with the piece, but I was sure I didn't like it. And yet by my senior year of high school, it had become the riptide that dragged me out to a sea of modern American music in which I still tread water. Now I hum it while walking down the street.

We, as ambassadors, must take nothing for granted, and avoid the assumption that our programs are either commonplace or radical. Rather, we have the chance to make everything we play new, every time, creating from nothing an experience, a path, a riptide. Our assumptions are just that, guesses and fantasies, including the assumption that someone who disrupts a concert hates the music. Some people laugh at funerals.

The last piece I performed on Saturday was Cage's 'silent,' most notorious and perhaps best-known work, *4'33"*. No one made a peep.

VERMONSTER

In high school, I worked at Ben & Jerry's. For the first six months or so, my mother drove me to work and picked me up afterward, which means I had to be 15. Within a year, I earned a promotion to "shift leader," meaning I served as a temporary manager during my shifts, which astounds me to this day. A beacon of responsibility, I was not. I would often get high with co-workers on the roof after work while chowing down on brownies, ice cream and cookies. One New Years Eve, I invited so many friends to the store that the Associated Press called to see if they'd missed something. "Is Ben & Jerry's throwing some kind of New Years Eve event?"

The scoop shop in Montpelier no longer exists, and I worked there before the company's acquisition by Unilever. At the time, the pints still had the old design, and the flavors, many short-lived, seemed as capricious as ever ("Peanut Butter and Jelly," anyone?). We'd do bottle drives for women's shelters and I would run the projector for outdoor movies. A massage therapist once came in to treat the whole staff.

Ben & Jerry's did, for all intents, fire me. It was my senior year and I'd left my shift to go play a quick performance at my high school—a Chopin etude, I still remember—and didn't sign out, while leaving a non-shift leader alone in the store. It was winter, the place was dead, and everything was fine, but I fucked up.

Anyway one day, well before my termination, a group of tourists came in and ordered a Vermonster, which is something like twenty scoops of ice cream, layers of cookies and brownies, any toppings the customer wishes, and of course whipped cream. I can't remember if we had cherries. And we would serve this insane thing in a plastic souvenir bucket. Usually sports teams would order the sundae after a game and share it, but still, for all the hype and fascination, the Vermonster was a rare bird. I only made a couple in all my time at Ben & Jerry's.

So this group of tourists came in and ordered their Vermonster. I dutifully scooped the ice cream, crumbled the cookies and brownies, tossed in the gummy bears and Reese's Pieces and whatever else they asked for, and covered it all in whipped cream and sprinkles. I handed them the bucket with a fistful of spoons. "Enjoy!"

About twenty minutes later, one woman from the group returned with the pale nearly empty but for a layer of goopy melted ice cream, fudge, caramel and masticated toppings. This was always the tough part, and just looking at that bucket of backwash turned my stomach. I knew what was coming: she would want me to wash that sludge out and return the clean bucket as a souvenir.

"Could you scrape what's left into that blender and add some milk?"

"Excuse me?"

"We'd like you to make it into a shake."

I asked for clarification again, and again, until she confirmed the unthinkable. "We want to drink it."

Gag reflex screaming, I took a spatula to the bucket and emptied the brown slime into a blender, added ice and milk, and hit the switch. Then I poured the ooze into a cup, popped in a straw and handed it over the counter. "Enjoy!"

ON BEING CALLED A FAGGOT, LIKE, ALL THE TIME IN NEW YORK CITY

I have a serious question for you: is the way I look at my phone gay? I only ask because earlier today on a downtown 6, I was standing there crafting a press release on my phone when a guy got on at 23rd Street, promptly muttered the word "faggot," and then sat in front of me. Standing there—quite buttoned-up, as it were, on my way to teach—I wondered if what just happened had actually just happened. Did I imagine him regarding me upon his entrance, before making that (so very) effortless acknowledgment? Did I imagine his disdainful glare continuing at that very moment?

I stared back, hoping he'd say it again. Then I'd know for sure. Then I'd say something. Then I'd be the radical queer activist I had imagined myself becoming, especially over the last couple weeks since the Pulse shooting in Orlando, talking my big game on social media and over coffee to my friends. Then I'd put my "enough is enough" money where my mouth is. I had a couple sentences ready. They burned in my chest. I would finally stand up for myself.

But we remained deadlocked, and I remained swimming in equal-parts anger, doubt, and rationalizations.

Say it again!

But he didn't. I got off at Astor Place, expecting even then for him to repeat the word as I exited. I had sentences planned for that, too. But nothing happened. Maybe none of it happened. Maybe I'm going crazy.

I'd planned on grabbing a salad before teaching, but suddenly had lost my appetite. Maybe a smoothie? A gay smoothie? Fuck. See, this is what actually pisses me off—that mine is not a story of courage, but rather a story where the bad guy wins and I don't get a salad, where he goes on with his day unpunished and unembarrassed while my brain remains absolutely poisoned. In this moment, I don't feel like a faggot. I feel like a coward.

I actually get called a faggot quite a bit these days. Before New York, I lived in Texas and Indiana. Conservative states, right? It never happened once. (Growing up in Vermont, it happened regularly enough that I monitored the frequency like a scientist.) But since moving to the Big Apple, off the top of my head there was that time on a bike with one of my best friends near Chinatown, once on the sidewalk near Times Square (I bumped into one of those people handing out newspapers, so he called me a faggot), once coming out of the subway station at Union Square, another time on a subway in Brooklyn, and then the time on the Upper West Side while running to a friend's gig at a church.

More may come to me. Oh, a couple weeks ago, two blocks from my apartment in a convenience store. A kid wanted money, but I didn't have any cash. "Faggot."

I came away from these experiences the same way I came away from today, wondering honestly if I run gay, sit gay, ride a bike gay, bump into people gay, walk up the stairs gay, buy chips gay, type press releases into my phone gay. Do my straight friends get called a faggot when they, too, run down the street or type into their phone on the subway, or am I really, truly, just so gay that it seeps through my every movement, overwhelming my various forms of straight drag?

I also come away from these situations seething with anger. At myself, that is. I replay fantasies in my mind where I handle things differently, where I demand some kind of... no, not an apology, fuck that... but where I go into a kind of Steven Seagal mode and give these people just a small taste of the humiliation triggered in an adult like me when that word resurfaces after a bully-conditioned childhood once peppered with it.

Yes, every time it's shouted, growled or muttered in my direction, more than the chants and heckles that followed me through high school, I remember the whispers of an eighth grade boy a year older than me—his name was Tom—who would sit behind me on the school bus and coo between the seats that he was going to kill me. Woven into the tapestry of his promise was his name for me. "Faggot." Frozen in my seat, I didn't say a word. I wonder if he remembers.

tidepools

ABOUT THE AUTHOR

Adam Tendler is a concert pianist, writer, composer and concert curator. A Vermont native, he lives in Brooklyn, New York with his husband, Francesco. This is his second book. More at adamtendler.com

www.ingramcontent.com/pod-product-compliance
Lightning Source LLC
Chambersburg PA
CBHW032117090426
42743CB00007B/378